ONE WHO POSSESSES A WHY
FOR THEIR EXISTENCE CAN
ENDURE ANY HOW.

M.C.Bell.

I'm struck speechless by your generosity towards humanity and all you've given to others---your unfiltered wisdom serves a purpose reflected in your undaunted power expressed. What a powerful tribute you've created to heal the exponentially growing wounded and their losses. Everything life has handed you, you have been guided to LEAD. You are an inspiration. Your invaluable intentions are perfect in every aspect and dimension.

– ARMAND ASSANTE, Legendary Actor

From the first glance at Michele's chart, the expansive and innovative aura of her Aquarius rising is reminiscent of Walt Disney's imaginative spirit. Her persona radiates a childlike aura of love, offering warmth in today's tumultuous times. Michele, is an intuitive philosopher, she delivers universal messages that demand attention. Her planets' grounded energies, steadfast and dedicated, anchor the profound wisdom she shares. Like the stars that navigate us through the cosmos, Michele's writings serve as a celestial guide through the landscapes of healing. Her essence celebrate the perpetual cycles of transformation and enlightenment while providing solace.

– JENNY LYNCH, Celebrity Astrologer

Foundation of
EMBRACE

Prelude to Stage One

This foundational section provides a comprehensive overview of *The 7 Stages of Grief*, setting the stage for the deep dive into **EXPRESS** that follows. While it serves as an introduction, it is designed to be revisited, offering insight and context as you navigate through each stage of your journey.

The EMBRACE Journey
Transform Grief and
Discover Inner *Strength*

Welcome, Warriors, to the extraordinary dimension of the 7 Stages of Grief Workbook Journal. I will guide you through a miraculous and empowering passage, unveiling the hidden treasures amidst the labyrinth of trauma and loss.

This course was born from my authentic desire to *heal it forward* in the grief community, ignited by theta meditation and a deep desire to manifest growth and healing through my writings. Drawing upon my intuitive theta-visions, I have created the EMBRACE framework — a radiant constellation of seven stages illuminating our transformative expedition in the wake of adversity.

In contrast to conventional approaches that merely skim the surface of emotions within the limited confines of the five stages of grief, I sensed the dire need for a holistic and transformative tapestry. The 7 stages of grief, meticulously crafted through my Healing it Forward modalities used in my 1:1 sacred retreats, transcend the ephemeral realm of emotions, ushering us into a realm where storytelling, the sacred utterance of our beloved's name, and the cultivation of gratitude mingle, guiding us through each challenging obstacle that graces our path.

Within this cherished community of kindred souls, we will unite, bound by a shared mission to collaborate, share our truth, and breathe life into one another's spirits—a sacred alchemy that fosters a radiant cascade of healing and metamorphosis. The modalities unveiled in the EMBRACE workbook journal's resplendent pages revolutionized how we navigate our sacred inner landscape, transforming the lives of those who have an unwavering longing to embrace the transformative work ahead.

As an extraordinary boon, I invite you to journey beside me as a Certified Grief Wellness Warrior, armed with the profound and purposeful modalities needed to extend a gentle hand to those ensnared in the clutches of their grief. By immersing yourself in these transformative practices and obtaining certification, you shall illuminate the path for others in their darkest moments, serving as a beacon of light and hope amidst the unfathomable abyss.

With deepest gratitude and genuine admiration, I extend my heartfelt appreciation to you for summoning the courage to embark upon the sacred journey of the EMBRACE workbook journal course. I assure you, Warriors, that this decision shall cascade with blessings and profoundly resonate. Together, let us traverse the infinite depths of grief, unlocking the wellspring of our inner fortitude and embarking upon a journey that transcends healing alone—a voyage brimming with purpose, renewal, and the willful power of the human spirit.

Prepare yourself for the transformational power of the 7 Stages of Grief Workbook Journal.

Let our extraordinary odyssey begin.

The Grief Warrior

Table of Contents

FOREWARD

My name is Cristal Sampson, and I work in mental health and psychiatry as a nurse practitioner in the UK, Connecticut, and New York, specializing in traumatic stress and mood disorders. I am also a young woman who experienced an early-term spontaneous miscarriage that burned a hole in depths I had previously not known existed. The revelation of this new depth of unconditional love, coupled with my baby's teeny heart stopping, left me hollow.

Even in my subsequent pregnancy the following year, I still felt empty of the unfulfillable desire for the baby back that I had lost in this life. The emptiness was filled with sadness, anxiety, and disappointment from troubled family dynamics – *a family unaware of my loss and grief.*

Someone with my expertise is never immune to the heartaches of the human experience, such as the loss of love and life. I recognized the potential to become an emotionally absent mother to my unborn baby, a fate that seemed all but certain at the time – and the thought terrified me. I am grateful to have understood that both my baby and I deserved the opportunity to heal. In my research, I discovered Michele, The Grief Warrior®.

As a health professional and a mental health specialist, I am particularly discerning about the services I opt for and the providers I choose. During this chapter of my life and given the circumstances, I did not pursue "traditional" mental health counseling. At that moment, confronting the challenges presented by contemporary therapy seemed beyond my capacity. I perceived the potential for a more conventional approach to be beneficial later in my healing journey.

What Michele provided touched the very core, breadth, and depth of my pain, reaching deep into the spiritual, mental, emotional, and energetic aspects of my being, body, and environment through a one-on-one retreat. I have not encountered anything like it since. Therefore, I am deeply moved that you are here, exploring the 7 Stages of Grief. Your journey with Michele's intentional energy, as conveyed through her books, and her custom human design modalities coupled with her healing energy, will extensively shift your essence and transform you.

FOREWARD

The *'EMBRACE: The 7 Stages of Grief'* workbook series is designed to support every individual navigating grief—those who feel unprepared and overwhelmed by the complexities of losing a loved one. This series speaks to the heart of those oscillating between the anticipation of loss and the necessity of maintaining 'normalcy,' amidst the swirl of anger, resentment, and sorrow. It is a compassionate companion for every silent sufferer, for those caught in the emotional storm of impending loss, and for caregivers in dire need of nurturing themselves.

What distinguishes Michele's *'The 7 Stages of Grief'* series most is the infusion of practical hope within its pages—a hope that is both tangible and deeply rooted in the natural spaces where resilience and healing begin. Michele brings a deep understanding and mastery in guiding others through the vast resources available for grief support, offering pathways that are both practical and easily navigable. Her insight into the caregiver journey, as a single mother is profoundly intimate, shaped by her own experience of lovingly supporting her teenage son, through his transition, enveloped in a cocoon of love. This unique perspective enriches her approach, making her guidance not only informed but deeply empathetic to the nuanced experiences of grief.

My work with Michele has caused a seismic shift in my perspective and has improved my relationships with myself, my family, and the people who meet me. I am moved with infinite gratitude at the positive and priceless impact my work with Michele has had on my experience of motherhood and the beautiful relationship my daughter and I get to have. Now, I enjoy expanding my connection as she has become a selfless friend and true mentor.

I encourage you to allow this book to transform you positively. Let it be a daily source of support and comfort, especially in moments of need. Remember, everything Michele has undertaken since Nicky's return to the Source has been a heartfelt ode to him and a homage to the enduring legacy of love and purpose he entrusted to her. Michele's ultimate wish is for you to discover your purpose and allow it to drive you forward through the cherished journey of your life.

Cristal Sampson

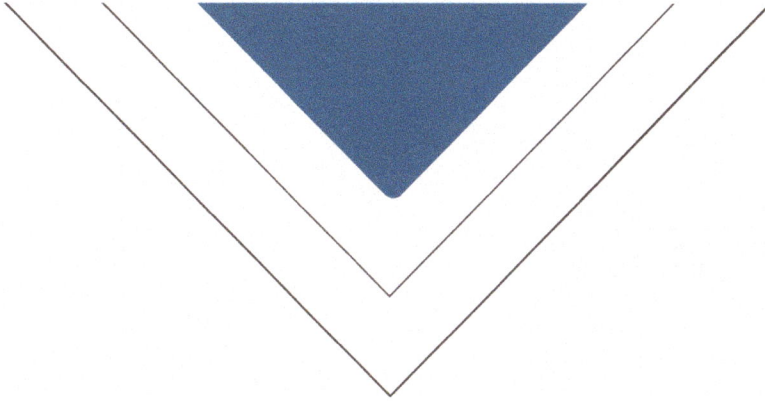

FROM MY HEART
to yours...

Alignment in the face of loss is the only option. When we open ourselves to the possibilities presented to us, we find this harmony: in the strength of our words, in the peace of our meditations, in the gift of our presence, in the renewal of our bodies, in the stirring of our spirits, in the depth of our relationships, and in the nourishment we give ourselves.

The path to recovery is a beautiful tapestry that offers the opportunity for personal development and the forging of inner fortitude. We will brave new territory together, learn new things, and grow as people. I will be your guide and source of solace throughout our journey together. Get ready to reclaim your life with renewed confidence as you learn to swiftly navigate life's complications and unleash your remarkable inner potential.

There is nothing scary or complicated about this course since I will be there to guide you through every one of the steps. Let's take off on a journey into the unknown, where the payoff to SELF could be infinite.

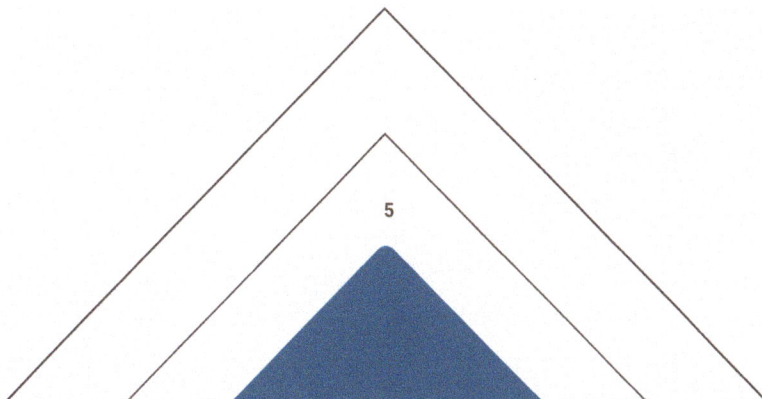

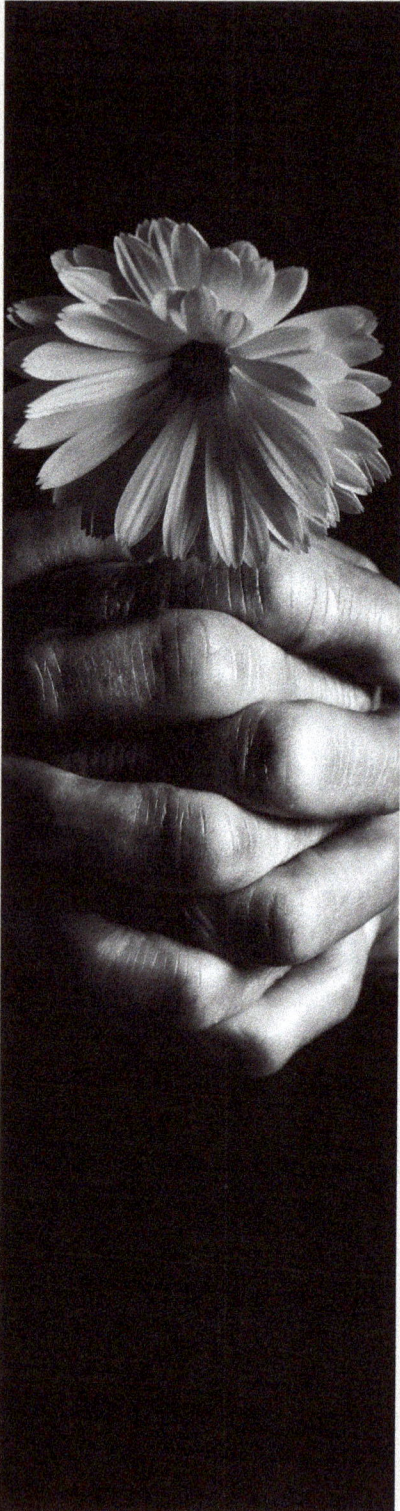

PROLONGED GRIEF DISORDER
Unveiled
as total B.S

Shattering the Illusion: Liberating Ourselves from the Constraints of the "5 Stages of Grief"

Adhering to established norms is a delusion, a fallacy we must quickly let go of when dealing with extended grief disorder. The "5 Stages of Bereavement" model developed by psychologists has been widely disseminated for too long, permeating every aspect of grief counseling and education.

Unfortunately, the constant push to conform to a set and narrow path of grieving has led me and countless other seekers within the grief community to feel disillusioned.

I beg you to disregard this erroneous advice immediately. The core meaning of our name, "EMBRACE," contains the whole truth. The concept of "Prolonged Grief Disorder" is 100% bogus.

The "5 Stages of Grief" concept originated from an unsupported theory meant to characterize the reaction of people who had been given fatal diagnoses rather than those who were navigating the maze of loss and sorrow. Here we have two utterly dissimilar yet actual experiences, each of which calls for special attention and comprehension.

UNVEILING THE TRUTH

The Evolution from 5 Stages of Grief to Prolonged Grief Disorder

In March 2022, a new grief-related disorder was officially adopted into mainstream mental health diagnosis nomenclature. Seeing how the clinical world has further shamed the sacred grieving world is disheartening. DSM-5's trauma and stress-related category have a new label: Prolonged Grief Disorder, created deliberately to define what grief should and should not look like.

But first, let's take a moment to think. What exactly is this thing called "Prolonged Grief Disorder"? Claiming a year for adults and a paltry six months for children is an arrogant attempt to restrict the complex fabric of grief inside the confines of time. According to the American Psychological Association, persons who carry this label are assumed to exhibit the following symptoms even after the diagnostic window has closed:

- The crushing weight of grief pressed down on every aspect of their being.
- An unending fixation on sorrow as memories of the lost reverberate ceaselessly.
- A mental panorama obscured by agony or the unsettling absence of feeling.
- They engage in a delicate dance of denial and avoidance as they try to face their loved one's death.
- Dissonance and disconnection can develop when one feels different from the social norm.
- Every breath is filled with the haunting repercussions of despair and isolation.

We stand at the intersection of societal, cultural, and religious expectations, where the mere fulfillment of established criteria has become pivotal in making a prognosis. Understandably, when engulfed by the darkness of losing a loved one, such clinical classifications may not bring the peace and comprehension one wants.

To promote genuine healing, we need to permit ourselves to explore our inner emotional landscape freely.

Let us stand up as one in our resolve to overcome this stereotype's obstacles. Let us regain our freedom from societal norms to grieve and heal as we see fit.

We will overcome obstacles as a group and EMBRACE the journey of getting to the heart of our pain and reclaiming our ways forward in healing.

WHY PROLONGED GRIEF DISORDER
is Facing So Much Criticism

01

There is no moral compass in the arena of mourning.

Grief isn't reducible to a single feeling but incorporates many of them. It weaves a complex and ever-changing mosaic of emotions, including sadness, rage, anguish, loneliness, reverence, connection, and perplexity.

It's a shared adventure that everyone does on their terms.

Grief is complex and multifaceted: No two souls mourn alike, for no two losses are identical. Attempts to confine the grieving process within cookie-cutter stages, rigid criteria, and prescribed timelines propagate the fallacy of a right or wrong way to grieve.

02

Grief, in its essence, is a natural phenomenon—

A sacred dance that unfolds within the depths of our being. It is a deeply personal and profound experience, far from being a pathological problem to be solved.

A child's heart carries the imprint of a parent's absence for months or years. Similarly, a parent's longing for a child, partner, or loved one transcends all notions of time. The ache, the longing, lives in the very essence of our human nature.

03

Grief is an enigmatic path; Grief isn't linear.—

If we were to create a line graph of our grief journeys, it would be surprising for scientists to discover no discernible pattern.

Within the ebb and flow of our grief, we encounter good and bad days interwoven in a twisted dance.

Embracing this is how we move with our grief. Labeling and attempting to confine it only breeds resistance. Progress lies *not* in imposing a specific timeline but in surrendering to the ever-changing flow of our grief and learning to move on with acceptance and dignity.

04

Grief isn't inherently harmful.

Grief is evidence of love lost.

It serves as a poignant symbol of our love, our desire to cherish and remember those individuals and relationships that hold deep significance in our lives.

It's instinctively human: both beautiful and painful. By labeling grief as a problem In this sacred space, By labeling grief as a problem to solve, we carry it. By leaning into our pain, we *move with* it.

05

Grief looms of isolation. Support becomes our lifeline.

Grief defies measurement, transcending the confines of milestones as the 5 Stages of Grief imply. It is an ever-evolving journey, an ongoing experience. Pathologizing and diagnosing grief makes it feel abnormal. In reality, it represents so much of the human experience.

Diagnoses can empower us by illuminating how our minds or bodies function differently and offering solutions. However, diagnosing grief only deepens the shame, loneliness, and isolation. No one should feel wrong for grieving beyond a specific date.

We need grief support, not grief diagnosis. By creating space for its expression, allowing its capacity to unfold without restraint.

Unlock the Profound Power of Healing with EMBRACE
The 7 Stages of Grief Alignment

Are you prepared to immerse yourself on a journey of healing and self-discovery?

Step into a sphere of authenticity, truth, and love as you immerse yourself in the unparalleled wisdom and guidance offered in the transformative EMBRACE course. This course goes beyond the ordinary, offering a depth of healing that will leave an indelible impact.

What sets EMBRACE apart? It emerges from the heart of an expert grief practitioner, infused with the spirit of authenticity and infused by a genuine desire to empower and support individuals on their unique healing journeys.

EMBRACE offers a transformative approach that transcends traditional teachings.

Through this meticulously crafted course, you will unlock the tools and techniques to navigate the depths of grief, embracing healing and growth. The 7 Stages of Grief Alignment workbook becomes your trusted companion, providing compassionate guidance through each stage. It empowers you to honor your journey, embrace your emotions, and pave the way for a purposeful shift.

However, EMBRACE's path forward still needs to be completed. Those interested in learning more and becoming certified "Healing it Forward" practitioners will find that this course provides a beautiful opportunity to do just that. As a trained professional, you will be honored to assist others on their journey to wholeness and personal development.

The EMBRACE program is an astonishing journey of self-discovery and empowerment, not simply another healing class. It encourages you to look within, where you'll find the key to your inner wisdom and the key to your recovery. Along the journey, you'll be surrounded and transformed by a community of like-minded spirits who share your unyielding dedication to growth and give support and encouragement.

Are you prepared to take your life's most incredible life-changing healing journey? Join us on this life-altering adventure, where our north stars are sincerity, honesty, and love. Learn the true meaning of pivoting with intent through your experience with EMBRACE. Your healing journey awaits, and we are here to walk alongside you every step of the way.

Are You Ready?

ALL RIGHT, GRIEF WARRIORS:

We're breaking up with the 5 Stages of Grief

Meet your new boo,
the 7 Stages of Grief Alignment!

The 7 Stages of Grief Alignment knows no order. They are not
steps but continual pillars, symbols, and actions to make
space for grief in your growth.

*Words hold immense power, and we choose to
transform our grief rather than diagnose it.*

The Grief Warrior

EMBRACE

THE 7 STAGES OF GRIEF ALIGNMENT

01

EXPRESS
Let your emotions guide you and experience the joy and fulfillment of expressing your true self through journaling and artistic exploration.

02

MEDITATE
Embrace the power of sitting with your grief, opening your heart, and leaning into the serenity of the present moment, creating space for healing and growth.

03

BE PRESENT
Pause. Observe and relinquish the need for constant busyness, and tune into the depths of your feelings. Embrace the beauty, opportunity, and purpose in this moment.

04

REJUVENATE
Reignite your zest for life, nourish your soul, and elevate your vibrations through the transformative power of self-care. Rediscover what it means to feel truly alive.

05

AWAKEN
Awaken the part of you that's been hiding. Reclaiming lost joy, energy, and vibrance. Rediscover the essence of your true self, waiting to be revealed.

06

CONNECT
Grief can separate us from true ourselves, making us feel like trapped observers of our lives, Reconnect physically, mentally, and spiritually to find your center and regain a sense of control and profound connection.

07

EAT HEALTHY
Nourish your body with the fuel it craves for strength and vitality. Embrace the sensory delight of flavors, textures, and intuitive connection as your body receives each healthy bite.

What 'stage' speaks to you?

IF YOU'RE READY TO TURN YOUR PAIN INTO FUEL...

Your past can lead you to your purpose.

Your pain can become your fuel to embody and fulfill that purpose. It's time to heal the resilient spirit within you, the one who has overcome more than imagined possible.

Unclench your jaw. Let out a sigh of relief - and stop running. We can't change our pasts. e may not alter our pasts, but we can find peace in our history and shape our futures by nurturing our souls in the present moment.

Each of us possesses a unique narrative shaped by our experiences. While we may not always have control over the plot, we have the power to choose the underlying theme. Let us craft our stories around the essence of healing rather than being defined by pain.

Rise as a warrior, not just a survivor. I am here to guide you because I believe in your strength.

It's time to take hold of the reins and chart a path toward healing, love, and inner strength.

i believe in you.

Your past paves the path to purpose.

Grab a pen, and we'll embark on your new journey together.

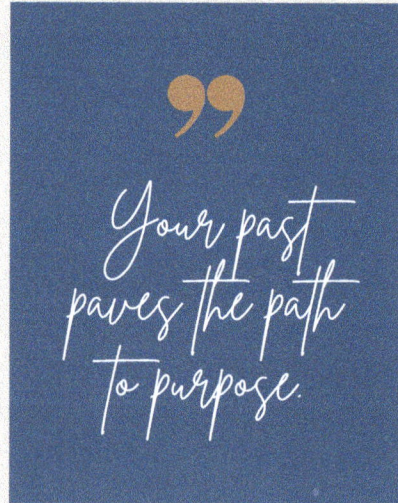

PIVOT *with* PURPOSE

My vocation is a sacred calling, where every word, line, and page is carefully crafted with intention and purpose. My vocation extends far beyond the conventional realms. It transcends the boundaries of traditional academia and ventures into the realm of energy and transcendence.

Having traversed the depths of deep trauma and loss, I intimately understand the weight of grief and despair. Yet, I alchemize that suffering into meaning through the art of writing, creating, and teaching. I am fueled by authentic and intentional love in every breath of my life.

It is not a love born out of obligation but a love that empowers and inspires, beckoning others to rise above their fears and embrace the limitless possibilities that lie within them.

To me, this is the very essence of sacredness.

Let this inspire you that, no matter your challenges, you can *Pivot with Purpose* and manifest life in alignment with your highest energy. As your Grief Warrior® mentor, I will guide you on a sacred transformation journey.

The Grief Warrior

I HAD TWO CHOICES:
Retreat Or Renew

When my first-born son passed away, grief consumed me. I could have withdrawn from life, but a fire within me refused to give up. It was then that I realized grief is the expression of love. It's our mind and heart's way of grappling with loss. It requires embracing the unknown, for life itself is unpredictable, regardless of our beliefs.

In rediscovering the magic of life, I rekindled my commitment to live truly. The grief didn't vanish, but it became more manageable. I started noticing the small things that bring joy to life. Each day became an adventure filled with endless possibilities. With an open heart, I welcomed the uncertainties that came my way. While the aftermath of a loss can leave us feeling hopeless, the strength to persevere can lead to unexpected achievements. Withdrawing may seem tempting, but it only perpetuates a downward spiral. We can move forward and rediscover joy by renewing our commitment to purposeful living.

I crafted the 7 Stages of Grief Alignment to renew my commitment—a guide from eleven years of personal experience and introspection. My book, A Son's Gift, became a testament to living intentionally after unforeseen circumstances. This challenge navigates the unexpected tragedies that may befall us, particularly if we face intense grief for the first time. Each stage holds significance, and we must traverse them daily. It isn't always easy, but a life infused with meaning and purpose is worthwhile.

Our Joyful Ending
Pain Meets Healing

Once upon a time,

...in the whimsical land of Serenityville, a group of courageous warriors known as the Serene Seekers set forth on a remarkable quest—the Journey of Healing it Forward. Guided by the wise and enchanting fairy Seraphina, they discovered the secret power of acceptance. The goal was to align with the 7 Stages of Grief and release the mystical power inside.

The Serene Seekers set out on their journey full of bravery and love. As they wandered through enchanted forests and sparkling waterways, they experienced times of hardship. They didn't shy away since they knew the answer to their problems resided within themselves.

The Serene Seekers blazed a trail based on the ancient wisdom of the 7 Stages of Grief Alignment. Each phase—"Express," "Meditate," "Be Present," "Rejuvenate," "Awaken," "Connect," and "Eat Healthy"—held a vital piece of the puzzle to their recovery and development.

Under Seraphina's guidance, the Serene Seekers learned that pain was not their enemy but a teacher to be embraced. It became a part of their story, a testament to their courage and resilience. United in their journey, they supported one another, sharing stories and offering solace when needed. Their empathy and compassion wove a love web across Serenityville.

By embracing their pain, the Serene Seekers discovered the profound magic of healing it forward. They realized their healing could inspire and uplift others, spreading hope and resilience far and wide.

The Serene Seekers' journey through the 7 Stages of Grief Alignment showcased the power of acceptance and showed the world how beautiful it can be. Their travels exemplified the concept of "healing it forward," the idea that one person's kindness may positively impact others.

And so, the Serene Seekers continued their noble quest, fueled by determination and love. Together, they embarked on the Journey of Healing It Forward, embracing their pain, sharing their stories, and spreading seeds of healing throughout Serenityville and beyond.

This uplifting tale illustrates the power of facing our suffering and moving with "Healing it Forward.

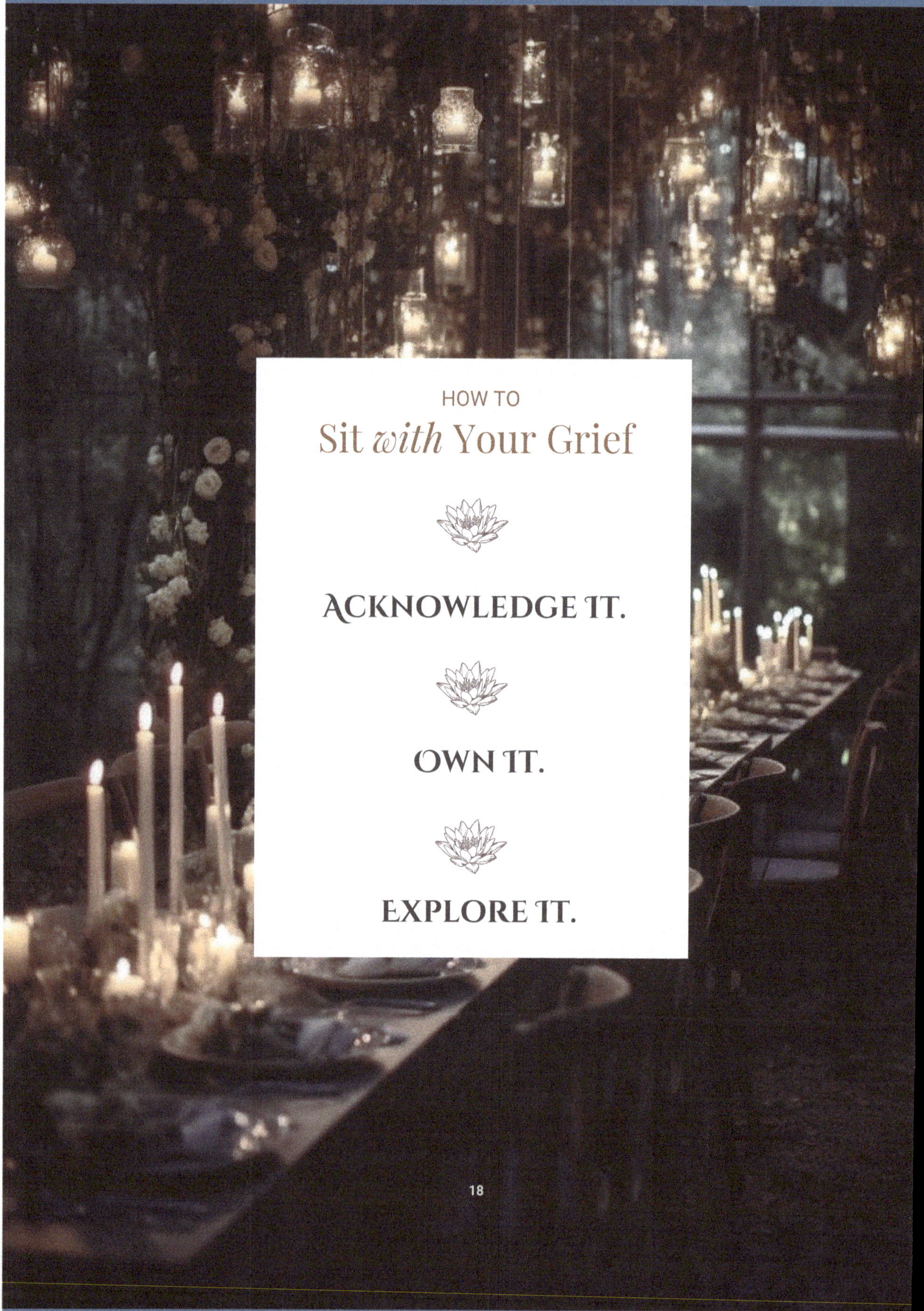

HOW TO

Sit *with* Your Grief

ACKNOWLEDGE IT.

OWN IT.

EXPLORE IT.

THERE ARE 3 FUNDAMENTAL

STEPS TO EMBRACING YOUR GRIEF

FEEL *and*
ACKNOWLEDGE IT

Feel - Dive into the Depths of Emotion In the first step. We will learn the art of feeling. Relax your body and mind by closing your eyes and taking a few slow, deep breaths. Don't oppose or judge the feelings you're experiencing.

Are you on the verge of purging, overwhelmed by a storm of pain, guilt, shame, betrayal, or envy?

In EMBRACE, you will understand the depth of your pain through emotional exploration. Embracing our feelings shows respect for the integrity of our experience and lays the foundation for healing.

To *acknowledge* is to embrace the power of acceptance with the courage to feel. It is easy to dismiss our grief, burying it beneath layers of denial or self-judgment. But this step teaches us to embrace our pain by acknowledging its presence. Let go of the urge to push your feelings aside or berate yourself for struggling. Instead, recognize that grief is a natural and valid experience. When you own your suffering, you allow yourself the time and perspective to determine what's causing it.

OWN YOUR FEELINGS
of Pain, Grieving, Loss

Understanding your feelings is the first step, but owning your pain is crucial. Grief is often associated with a side of ourselves that we prefer to ignore, so we dismiss it. However, pushing your emotions aside or criticizing yourself for struggling can worsen things. Instead, it's essential to accept your pain as a natural and valid experience and take responsibility for it.

By holding yourself accountable, you can create the space and understanding necessary to delve deeper into the issue and uncover its root cause. This process of self-exploration allows you to work with your pain rather than fighting against it, leading to gradual healing and release from its grasp. With time, you may find that your pain becomes a source of wisdom and inspiration, helping you cultivate self-compassion, acceptance, and strength.

So, don't dismiss your pain or judge yourself for feeling it. Embrace it as an opportunity for self-discovery and growth, and let it guide you on your journey.

ARE YOU LIVING A LIFE *of Denial*?

Denial is a tempting refuge, an escape from facing the truth that awaits us. But is it truly living?

Yet, in denying our true selves, we rob life of its vibrant colors. We become sleepwalkers, traversing existence without truly seeing or experiencing its wonders. Disconnected from our emotions, we numb ourselves to the essence of our being, avoiding the aspects of life we dare not confront.

Grief has a way of leaving us feeling empty, disconnected from the world. Faced with such turbulent emotions, it is crucial to remain present. Opening ourselves to the surrounding reality allows us to reestablish our connection to ourselves and the world surrounding us.

If denial has become your shield for too long, it is time to confront the truth. Though it may be a painful pilgrimage, evading your emotions and sidestepping the obstacles that impede your growth will only perpetuate your suffering. To live a life of integrity and authenticity, we must be brave enough to acknowledge our wounds and fears.

Embrace the journey, for it may come with its share of challenges. Remember, transformation is not an overnight process; it requires time and intense dedication. But as you courageously confront your pain, you will uncover hidden wells of strength within. Say goodbye to denial and welcome the truth of your existence. With each intentional step, you carve a path toward a life filled with authenticity and purpose.

The path ahead may be arduous, but you are not alone. I am here to offer my unwavering support, accompanying you through every stride of this transformative journey. Embrace your inner resilience and have faith in the healing process.

Trust yourself and step boldly into a life of authenticity and growth. You have the power to rewrite your story.

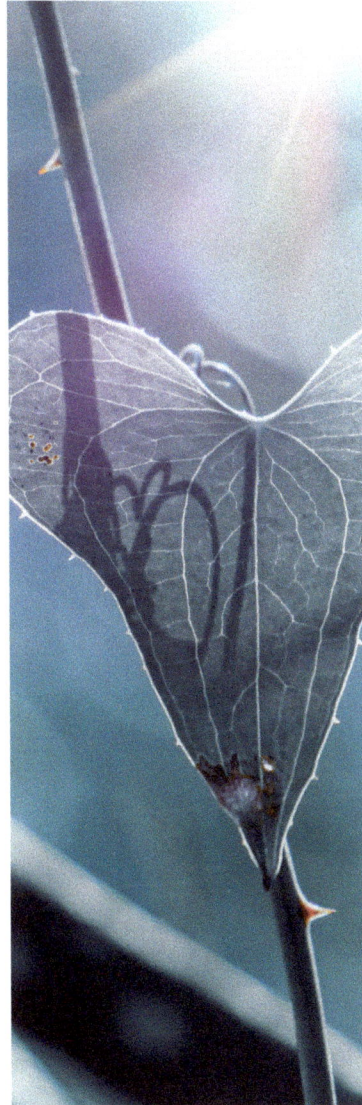

The Guiding Light of *Embrace* Nurturing Those in Grief

Faced with another's grief, we often find ourselves at a loss for words. The profound pain and sorrow they bear can leave us powerless, uncertain of how to offer solace in their darkest hours. Yet, amidst the vastness of this challenge, there exists a flare of hope—a well-crafted grief book, EMBRACE.

In these pages, you'll find a companion journal that will bring comfort and understanding to those roaming the twisted path of sorrow.

While it is impossible to erase the pain, EMBRACE can soothe the aching heart and guide one's steps through the obstacles of grief.

The sentimental narratives make the emotions' kaleidoscope more explicit and the burden of grief more tolerable. As a treasured tool in your grief bag, the 7 Stages of Grief Alignment provides a roadmap for the griever and their companions, fostering awareness and healing.

Yet, it is crucial to remember that when supporting someone living in grief, the gift of your presence and enduring willingness to listen outweighs any words of wisdom or reassurance.

With its intricate nuances, grief often leaves those who mourn feeling isolated and misunderstood. EMBRACE is a heartfelt promise that assures you that you are not alone in your journey.

EMBRACE will offer hope and encouragement, reminding readers they are not alone in their sorrow. Consider giving them a copy to support a friend or loved one during grief.

If you want to support a friend or loved one during grief, consider giving them a copy of EMBRACE! You want the support of your loved ones, and the same goes for them needing you. As with any journey in life, the journey of grief as a team, we got this!

The Healing Dance of Grief
Nurturing the Spirit *within*

When someone close to us dies tragically, we are engulfed by an overwhelming sense of loss, accompanied by a symphony of painful emotions. We journey through this dimension of grief, uniquely navigating its twists and turns. Some shed tears like raindrops from a stormy sky, others ignite with fiery anger, while some retreat into the solitude of their inner world. These reactions, these expressions of grief, are the rivers that flow from the depths of our souls. We must honor them, for within these expressions lie the seeds of self-awareness and the catalysts for healing.

It's simple to feel disoriented and overwhelmed in today's fast-paced, ever-evolving society. The grieving process is a multifaceted test; we all long for the loving company of a compassionate that requires us to seek comfort from those who can relate. As a holistic practitioner, I stand ready with the tools and resources to accompany you on this sacred pilgrimage. Drawing upon my extensive experience, I offer a sanctuary where your voice can be heard, your story shared, and your healing ignited.

Discerning the way forward is exhausting in life's chaotic orchestra, where confusion and uncertainty reign. The weight of emotional pain may tempt us to forge ahead, mindlessly seeking an escape from the obstacles that hinder our progress. Yet, dear soul, a profound wellspring of resilience and strength lies within you. Developing spiritual growth can lead to a limitless abundance of peace and stability. Nurturing your connection with a higher power or the wisdom within you can help you navigate life's most brutal storms with grace and serenity. As you enter this sacred journey of spiritual expansion, you will uncover newfound capacities to navigate life's turbulent seas, supporting your passage and extending a loving hand to those who traverse similar paths.

The road may appear dimly lit as you tread its winding path. Yet, within you resides a radiance of faith, highlighting the darkness for those who desire comfort in your presence. Even when grief looms, keep hope alive in the sanctuary of your heart. I encourage optimism even in the darkness. Envision a shining star, your inner strength shining its light into the deepest crevices of despair. As you gaze upon the darkness, challenge fear and vulnerability to manifest and transform into a conduit for healing. By embracing the full spectrum of your being, shadows, and all, you control the destiny of self-empowerment. Even in the trenches of darkness, your intense light inspires and uplifts those who witness your strength and courage.

Remember that you are never alone in the sacred dance of grief, where each step is steeped with the essence of unconditional love. Reach out, Warrior, to those who can guide and support you on this transformative pilgrimage. Together, you will honor the pain, nurture your spirit, and spin a tapestry of healing that extends far beyond the realms of grief. Let the rhythm of your heart guide you, as it holds within it the tune of perseverance, the harmony of optimism, and the assurance of rejuvenation.

Shadows become tools that help shape Who You Are...

The Symphony of *Empathy* Navigating Responses to *Grief*

Have you ever felt alone in your sadness because others choose to ignore or withdraw from you?

It's disheartening to question whether you deserve support or understanding. It can be challenging for those not accustomed to dealing with intense emotions like grief to face their feelings. Fear, unfamiliarity, and a lack of knowledge about responding supportively could all contribute to their feelings.

It can feel like others are trying to hide from the truth of your experience and being when they avoid hearing about your sorrowful tale. It might make you feel invisible, alone, and desperate for approval. An essential part of the grieving process is vulnerability, which searches for comfort in human connection and comprehension.

However, it is essential to note that only some can face and hold space for strong emotions, especially if they have not experienced something comparable. Their insecurity stems from a need for more ease with showing emotion. It's important not to take their reaction personally; instead, give yourself time and space to work through your feelings.

Be gentle with yourself and embrace the understanding that not everyone will comprehend or offer enduring support on this path. With time, you'll meet people who can hold the sacred space for your grief, opening doors to vital life lessons and opportunities for new relationships.

There can be many reasons why people don't respond to your melancholy expressions. Some people may struggle with displays of intense emotion, while others may feel ill-equipped to respond to someone who is deeply sorrowful. In certain instances, people may even fear that witnessing your sadness will awaken their dormant pain. It is essential to acknowledge that each person uniquely navigates grief, and adverse reactions to your sorrow do not show a lack of care or concern. Give them breathing room to deal with their feelings; they may discover the strength to help you.

As you continue your grief journey, remember that your emotions are valid and that your need for support is real. Seek solace in those who can hold space for your grief, and let go of the notion that everyone will understand. The dance of empathy requires patience and calls for self-compassion. If you care for yourself during this process, you show others how accepting melancholy can strengthen the spirit.

The Whispers of *Compassion*
Nurturing *Empathy* Through Small Acts

Empathy's complex webs of connection strengthen relationships during the grieving process. A kind touch, reassuring words, and a listening ear can go a long way toward alleviating emotional pain. During sadness, expressions of sympathy transform into a beautiful melody of support, kindness, and concern.

Even the tiniest gestures can convey the magnitude of affection and concern in moments of quiet reflection. Sincerity and love injected into the most straightforward actions can illuminate the darkest places. These seemingly insignificant acts go beyond words to bring solace to the soul. By doing these nice things for them, we can let them know they have our undying support and are not alone.

Sometimes, the answer lies not in words but in the silent embrace of companionship. To stand beside someone in their darkest hours to honor their wishes can transcend an act of compassion. You become a sanctuary of support for their wounded soul. Becoming a lifeline amidst the chaos by offering practical help, running errands, and preparing nourishing meals demonstrates that our warmth extends beyond mere words to sacred stillness.

They provide a sympathetic ear that accepts their suffering without judgment or making demands. We become instruments of compassion and wisdom, holding the door open for their recovery.

When words fail, being there and knowing how grateful we are can help comfort a broken spirit. Therefore, let us recognize the significance of greeting cards, reassuring embraces, and quiet moments of reflection. Aim to personify empathy, compassion, and concern. We become the vessels through which comfort is delivered, mending the broken parts of a mourning person's spirit in those quiet times.

You can use the following phrases:

My heart goes out to you; I'm sorry this is happening to you.
"What is your loved one's name?"
"What do you say we get some lunch together? Please tell me more about (insert name of cherished one here)."

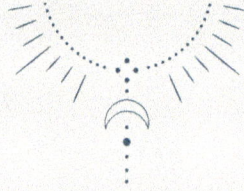

The Unseen Language of Sorrow
Embracing *Understanding* and *Letting Go*

It's frustrating when those close to you don't understand how much your loss means to you. Some wonder if avoiding those who can't share our sorrow is right. But let's PAUSE to think about this:

No matter how well you articulate your pain, not everyone can comprehend complex emotions. Despite our efforts to articulate our pain, some may struggle to grasp its true essence. In these situations, letting go of our dependence on their comprehension is not a sign of a lack of strength or inability. Our efforts to help them understand the inexplicable would be well-spent.

Don't you think it's wonderful to imagine a world where empathy is cultivated and understanding becomes a part of our collective etiquette? While that ideal may be far off, we can take comfort in the company of those who share our values and offer proper understanding and support. Seek comfort in knowing you are not alone on your grief journey. By doing so, we create space for our healing, allowing our sorrow to unfold in its way, guided by our resilience and the support of those who truly understand.

01

Let us find comfort in the arms of those who truly understand and share our pain on this developing path of sorrow. Even if others can't understand our pain, it's reassuring that some would listen with empathy and provide a safe place to heal.

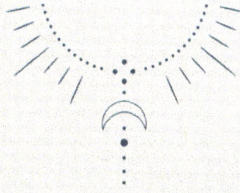

02

In the depths of sorrow, we are faced with a "griefosophical" lesson:

We are the chosen ones entrusted with the sacred duty of carrying the unseen language of sorrow. It is not a burden to bear but a calling that sets us apart from others. Our connection with our departed loved one runs deep, transcending the comprehension of others. The love we shared with them was unique, profound, and intimate, coloring our grief in hues that may mystify those who did not experience the same depth of connection.

Rather than harboring resentment or seeking understanding from those who cannot offer it, we can shift our perspective. It helps to think of ourselves as spiritual vessels that have solemnly promised to bear the burden of our grief. To mourn together is to witness the strength of love and reveal the depth of our connection.

By letting go of the expectation that everyone will understand our grief, we unlock a sense of communal understanding only discernible by our innermost beings. We become a collective source of higher consciousness. Our common grief language helps us bond with those who resonate with our vibe.

So, Warriors, Let up, hoping other people share your pain with you. Embrace the idea that you are connected to a group of people who "get it," and you become a force that cannot be stopped together. Make use of your suffering as a starting point for introspection and growth.

In doing so, you give tribute to the unconditional love you shared with your departed loved one and become that twinkle who walks this path of grief.

In grief, we are chosen to carry
the unseen language of sorrow,
a testament to our love and
resilience.

Unveiling the Art of
Respecting *Grief*

In this era of digital connectivity, we find ourselves conditioned to swiftly move on and brush aside the depths of our grief. Glossing over the importance of grieving and grief acceptance might be easy in today's fast-paced world. However, grief encompasses far more than prolonged sadness; it is an emotional journey that demands time, reverence, empathy, and patience to mend.

Loss, especially the irreparable loss of love, is at the heart of mourning. When we suffer a profound loss, it changes who we are and shines a light on what gives our lives true purpose. The path to recovery and growth lies in sincerely accepting our suffering.

Nobody enjoys being hurt, and most people will try to avoid it. However, suffering is a part of being human and must be faced head-on. Grief and loss, and the emotional sorrow they cause, are experiences all humans share at some point. Neither can we expect anybody else to take away our suffering, but we can show compassion, which can teach us a great deal about how to deal with the misery of others. Through compassion, we see that the suffering of others is natural and merits our whole attention.

The ability to empathize with others serves as a helpful reminder that there is no single "correct" way to deal with suffering. It is unnecessary to have all the solutions to be compassionate; all we need to do is be there for people when they are suffering.

So, when we see a loved one going through a tough time, let's not rush to ease their suffering. Instead, let's give our undivided attention to becoming wise. By doing so, we show them the kindness and consideration they deserve. There is an act of tremendous bravery, tenacity, and grit at the heart of mourning, an act that teaches profound truths about what it is to be human. So, let's not rush past the remembrances of limitless, unconditional LOVE.

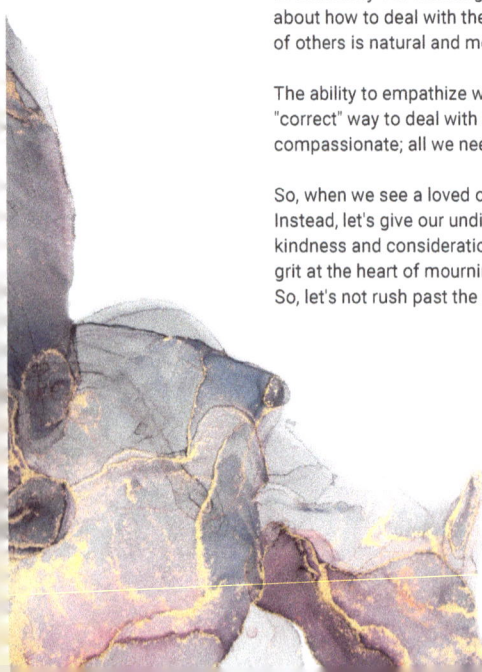

Embracing the *Everlasting* **Journey**

BOTTOM *line*

One of life's greatest challenges is coming to terms with the fact that mourning is never really "done." We may reach a point where the raw pain of our loss has begun to fade, but the scars remain. These scars can be a source of strength and comfort. They remind us of the loved ones we have lost and help us appreciate life's fragility.

But keep in mind that you will never fully "get over" your loss. It is an ongoing journey that we all must travel. There may be days when the path is smooth and the going is rough. But eventually, we will reach our destination: a place where we can find peace and happiness again.

Healing is an ever-unfolding journey, an intricate dance of self-discovery and growth. As we set out on our journey, we recognize that our wounds are not who we are but a testament to our capacity to love fiercely and persevere through adversity. Unconditional self-love feeds the soul and opens the door to healing on all levels. Putting aside baggage and focusing on what brings us joy might help us find inner freedom.

You may find that your relationship with your loved one changes as you move through grief. Their presence becomes a source of strength and comfort, reminding you of their eternal love. You gradually rebuild your life as you heal, carrying their memory within you. Their spirit entwines with yours, illuminating the path to a meaningful existence.

While healing may never be complete, grief can propel you toward a more positive emotional journey. Embracing and expressing your grief healthily allows for soul healing to begin.

express

meditate

be present

rejuvenate

awaken

connect

eat healthy

E
M
B
R
A
C
E

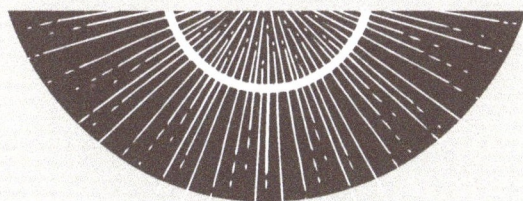

DOES EMBRACE
Speak to You?

Explore the transformative power of The 7 Stages of GRIEF Alignment workbook journal, designed to support you authentically and effectively on your grief journey. Each stage of this journal is carefully crafted to nurture your physical and mental well-being, empowering you to strengthen critical aspects of your health as you navigate through the aftermath of a traumatic event. Embracing these stages will lead you to greater strength, resilience, and a revitalized sense of purpose.

Drawing from personal experiences of loss and trauma, I created the 7 Stages of GRIEF Alignment mini journal to assist those willing to EMBRACE in their healing process. Within its pages, you'll discover practices that have deeply impacted my grief journey, enabling me to navigate through the pain and embrace genuine growth mindfully. These practices have brought about timeless healing, from releasing old attachments to rebuilding a lost sense of unconditional love.

This eternal healing perfectly captures the beauty of "Healing."

Whether at the beginning of your grief journey or making progress, embracing the stages outlined in this journal can ease the burden and infuse joy into your life. Let's say you've had enough and are ready to start living again. Please join me on the 7 Stages of the GRIEF Alignment workbook journal's transformational journey, or go even further and earn your Certified Wellness Warrior designation.

Take a deep breath, stay resilient, and remember that even in the darkest moments, we possess the inner strength to move forward. Embrace this opportunity and witness its profound impact on your life. Not doing so would be a mistake.

EXPRESS

Welcome to the First Stage of Grief Alignment: Express. In this stage, we encourage you to unleash your thoughts, feelings, and trauma through emotional journaling. By embracing this practice, you voice your emotions and release anxiety, triggers, and pain.

Reflect on its meaning in your grief journey and explore its significance. Use your notebook as a place of refuge where you may explore who you are and how you got here. Allow your own words to heal and shape your spirit.

Three ways you can integrate 'Express' into your daily therapy:

Emotional Journaling
Write freely each day to express and process your emotions.

Artistic Expression
Engage in creative activities to communicate and release emotions.

Verbal Communication
Share your feelings with a trusted person or practitioner for support and validation.

Expression is the key to unlocking our connection, allowing us to co-create a reality rooted in love and acceptance. So say their name, share your story, feel every moment, and remember—you are here for a reason. And always remember—you are here with a purpose. You have the power to create. So keep expressing yourself—you have everything it takes to thrive!

How will you express today?

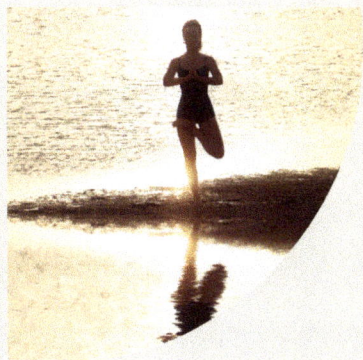

MEDITATE

Have you ever explored the richness of meditation? It offers a gateway to discovering tranquility and clarity in grief or challenging moments. By dedicating time to cultivating mindful awareness, we unlock the potential for remarkable revelations.
With each intentional inhalation and exhalation, we create a sacred space within ourselves, allowing us to confront our emotions from a higher perspective.

Discover peace in nature's embrace, where meditation unveils transformative insights.

Pause for a moment and ask yourself: When was the last time you truly paused and immersed yourself in the vivid reality of "here"? It is in the here and now, the ever-present moment, where true existence lives. It is within this moment that the miracle of life unfolds.

BE PRESENT

'Be Present' is the 3rd Stage of Grief Alignment, encouraging us to be still. Society often expects us to conform to specific standards, but we have the power to within ourselves begin a path toward wellness simply by showing up.

Being present allows us to reconnect with life, love, and feel again.

Let's focus on being present and mindful. Pay attention to your breath - feel the rise and fall of your chest and let it move like a symphony's crescendo. Focus on the present and feel the caress of each inhale and exhale. Take in the vibrant feelings that sweep your entire being, and let them merge with the present moment.

Allowing your emotions to take over can be liberating. Accepting and working with our feelings without hesitation or judgment is crucial. Whatever those emotions may be, it's okay to feel them. Take a moment to permit yourself to step back, allowing your soul to have time within this very breath.

REJUVENATE

For true revitalization, we must turn inward and examine our bodily, mental, and spiritual states.

It can help us reclaim our vitality and lead us toward joy and fulfillment, especially when dealing with the loss of a loved one or the constant stresses of modern life. Transformation comes with self-reflection, inner growth, and healing. You have the power to do this!

By embracing new challenges and striving to grow in every aspect of our lives, we can reignite the spark and fire up our souls. So, why wait? We can rejuvenate and awaken joy at every level with determination and self-acceptance.

Reflecting on our loved ones and the gifts they gave us can also help rejuvenate our lives in their honor. Whether remembering a favorite memory or reaching out to those who supported us during difficult times, each act deepens the connection between us and our loved ones, even as they move beyond the physical world.

Ultimately, we choose how to react to grief, but by acknowledging our journey and embracing joy, we can find strength in our spirit again.

AWAKEN

In the 5th Stage of Grief Alignment, Awaken, you are invited to embrace the essence of being fully alive and anchored in the present moment. Retaining and shielding ourselves from raw emotions and harsh realities is expected in the depths of grief.

Awakening is the key that unlocks the door to our inner resilience and rekindles our faith in the truth that lies before us.

Pause and contemplate your life as it stands today. Allow this fresh perspective to offer a broader view, enabling you to observe your journey from a distance. In this introspection, you may realize that all you need lives within, and a vast expanse of possibilities awaits you on the horizon.

Let's embrace the awakening, as it acts as a catalyst that propels us forward with a renewed sense of vitality and purpose on our journey.

CONNECT

In the 'C' of EMBRACE, we find the power of connection in the 6th Stage of Grief. As we make our way through the complexities of this world, now is the moment to strengthen our connection to ourselves, our spirit, and our mind. While it may pose challenges, remember that we all thrive on daily connections.

How will you choose to CONNECT today?

Your mind. Your body. Your spirit.

Make a conscious effort to connect with yourself by dedicating just five minutes to express gratitude, a walk in nature, engaging in reflective journaling, cooking, creating, or allowing yourself to be still. Focus on self-care and self-reflection to enhance your well-being.

Tune in to your needs and honor them, for it is in these connections that true healing and growth can flourish.

EAT HEALTHY

In the final stage of our grief alignment journey, we are called to embrace the importance of nourishing ourselves through healthy eating. As we have journeyed through the different stages of grief in our course, we have learned the significance of addressing our emotional, mental, and spiritual needs. Now, we focus on the physical aspect of our well-being, recognizing that what we put into our bodies directly impacts our healing process.

Eating healthy becomes the inner thread that weaves all the stages of our grief alignment journey. By nourishing ourselves with wholesome, nutrient-rich foods, we provide our bodies with the fuel to support our healing from the inside out. We actively participate in our healing process by prioritizing foods promoting strength, vitality, and well-being.

As we continue our journey beyond grief, let us carry healthy eating lessons. Let us embrace the power of wholesome foods to support our ongoing healing and growth.

It is through this holistic approach that we can truly thrive and create a life that is vibrant, nourished, and filled with joy.

YOUR INNER
spiritual warrior!

EMBRACE is the ultimate exhilarating journey of healing and transformation. This course is not just a certification—it is a profound commitment to healing and a powerful dedication to moving forward with purpose.

We encounter countless challenges that test our resilience and tempt us to give up. Yet, deep within us lies an untapped well of strength, waiting patiently to be discovered and unleashed. This course empowers you to tap into that inner strength, unlock your full potential, and become the vessel to *healing it forward*.

The key lies in listening to your heart and trusting your instincts. By tuning into the untapped wisdom at the core of your being, you gain the clarity and guidance needed to navigate any obstacle that comes your way. With a resilient focus, you cultivate the courage and determination required to **move with** emotional barriers.

As you EMBRACE this journey, you discover that nurturing your inner world positively impacts your external world, cultivating meaningful connections with others, and investing in your self-enlightenment. The key lies in listening to your heart and trusting your instincts.

The 7 Stages of Grief Alignment will be your guiding light as you EMBRACE each stage of grief in your own time. Recognize that these stages are not linear processes; you may move back and forth between them as you navigate your unique grief journey. This flexibility allows you to honor your experience and progress at your own pace.

Are you ready to step into your power as a Certified Grief Wellness Coach?
Sign up today and trust your inner calling, take that leap of faith, and let your guiding light illuminate the path of healing and transformation for yourself and others.

A Graceful Pivot to Purpose

you've made it

You are now ready to **EMBRACE** our First Stage:

express

That's the blessing and power of **pivoting with purpose.**

What are the 7 Stages of Grief Alignment?
Express. **M**editate.
Be Present. **R**ejuvenate.
Awaken. **C**onnect. **E**at Healthy.

Healing begins with acceptance, and alignment transforms us through embracing our circumstances.

The empower of embracing is in your next chapter –
are you ready to turn the page?

Table of Contents

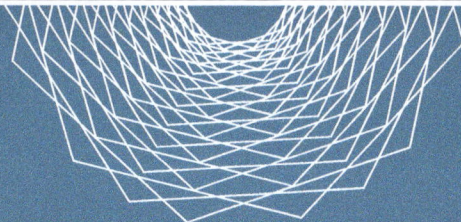

EXPRESS
our first step

Navigating through loss and grief is undeniably one of the most arduous journeys in a person's life. It is common to retreat and bury these emotions deep within instinctively. Yet, the weight of this burden doesn't dissipate with time unless addressed genuinely and compassionately. We genuinely require abundant love, expression, and mindful attention for healing.

Harnessing the Power of Writing for Healing During Grief

Accepting and acknowledging the emotions of grief is a vital step toward healing. You unlock the potential for profound transformation by actively listening to your feelings. Writing is a powerful tool in this journey, enabling a deeper understanding and appreciation of your emotions and fostering growth amidst the pain.

In this course, you will engage in transformative writing practices, authentically expressing your heartfelt feelings. Through this process, you will better understand your emotions, giving them the space they deserve. Embracing this healing practice, you embark on a journey of self-discovery, navigating the depths of grief and finding solace through understanding.

This course includes:

- Nine lessons – each including writing exercises and questions to self-reflect on
- Expert grief guidance and lessons on how to use writing to channel your feelings
- Guidance on how to write from the heart
- Tried and tested methods to move past the grief and heal
- Self-reflection on loss and where it has taken you

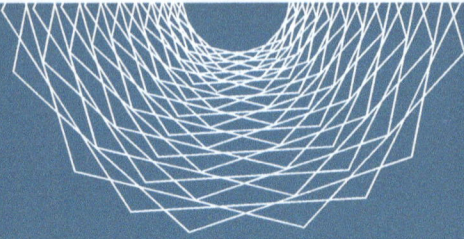

You should take this course if:

- ☀ You have painful and repressed memories
- ☀ You recently experienced a loss or grief
- ☀ You wish to understand your feelings better
- ☀ You want to learn how to use writing to FEEL
- ☀ You want to address the loss of a loved one
- ☀ You want to find peace

This interactive journal workbook is designed to help you express your feelings, providing a safe and nurturing space to articulate your pain, reflect on your experiences, and chart your progress toward healing. By using writing as an outlet, you'll be able to draw from your inner strength, transforming your energy into a powerful tool for healing.

❝

"I am Living Proof a Broken Heart Can Still Live"

The Grief Warrior

Write a mantra you can return to when you feel overwhelmed by grief.

_____

_____

_____

_____

"Say Their Name" in a quote.

_____

_____

_____

_____

LESSON 1 — How Writing Can Help *to* Heal Loss

Experiencing loss can profoundly affect every aspect of your life. The absence of a loved one can leave a void that seems impossible to fill. The mind grapples to understand the enormity of the loss; your heart yearns for the one who is no longer there; stress permeates your body; and your spirit may feel as though it's in a state of turmoil. Navigating this emotional landscape can be overwhelming.

Healing from such profound grief is a journey that takes time. There often comes a moment—a turning point—when the weight of the loss becomes too heavy to bear. At this juncture, the void begins to fill with love and peace. To reach this point of transformation, self-expression becomes a vital tool.

Understanding and articulating your feelings is the first step toward healing. Expressing these emotions through words can be incredibly therapeutic, transforming your pain into a catalyst for growth. Many find solace in writing, as it provides a private, peaceful, and intimate space for authentic self-expression that originates from the soul.

Writing is a holistic process that integrates your body, mind, spirit, and emotions, uniting them in a common goal: healing. It allows you to channel your pain, replacing it with positive energy as you journey toward overcoming your loss.

Writing is more than just moving your hand across a page. It's a deep dive into your emotions, memories, and sensory experiences. It's about transforming your life experiences into words, giving a tangible form to your grief and a pathway to healing. Embrace the power of writing and embark on your journey toward healing and peace.

> At every point in the human journey, We find that we have to let go in order to move forward; And letting go means dying a little. In the process, We are being created anew, Awakened afresh to the Source of our being.
>
> *Natalie Goldberg*

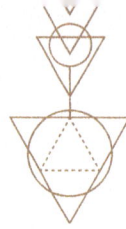

Once upon a time, in the heart of a storm called Loss, a mind was lost in a labyrinth of confusion, desperately seeking understanding and answers. As the storm began to subside, the mind transformed into a sanctuary, where answers slowly unfolded like the petals of a blooming flower.

Amid the storm, a heart reached out, yearning for the one taken too soon. As the skies cleared, the heart, like a skilled architect, began to rebuild itself piece by piece, each brick a testament to resilience and love.

Initially seeking shelter from the storm of stress, the body began to find its strength as healing took root. It transformed into a powerhouse, fueling the journey toward the dawn of healing. The spirit, initially lost in the storm's vastness, gradually found its way to become a lighthouse, radiating inspiration as the healing sun began to rise.

In this tale, *Pain*, the most disorienting and bewildering character, cannot be overcome by the body or mind alone. It required a collective effort to pool all inner resources and pull together towards a shared goal—the healing sunrise.

On this journey, writing emerged as a powerful ally. It empowered the characters to articulate their feelings, converse with the loved one they've lost, and dialogue with their past, present, and future selves. It allowed them to take control of their narrative and shape their memories and experiences into a story of resilience and growth.

What lessons can you embrace from this story?

Where did this story fit into the tapestry of their lives? Reflecting on these questions, let your thoughts flow.

if you haven't tried, you haven't lived

Letters of Love

All the writing for this course should be written in your Warrior Journal, a sacred space for your thoughts, emotions, and reflections. Your Warrior Journal is a sanctuary where your words can flow freely. It's a space to express your deepest feelings, knowing they will be held confidently. You can revisit your writings whenever you wish, to add to them, alter them, or even erase them. This is your journey, and your journal reflects your path.

Choose a serene and comfortable space for your writing sessions, away from the world's distractions. Let this be a place where you can focus on your thoughts and emotions, away from the interruptions of everyday life. Remember, there's no rush on this journey.

A Letter to Your Beloved:
A Heartfelt Beginning to Your Healing Journey

Take a deep breath, find a quiet space, and let your heart guide your pen. It's time to write a letter to your loved one. Begin with a simple, heartfelt salutation:

"Dear, My Love, My _____," and fill in the blank with the name of your loved one.

This is your moment to reconnect, reminisce, and express everything in your heart. Share your cherished memories, the moments that made you laugh, the times that brought you closer. Tell them what they meant to you, what they still mean to you. Let your words paint a picture of your shared journey, of the love that continues to live in your heart.

Don't worry about the perfect words, the perfect grammar, or the perfect punctuation. This is not about perfection; it's about expression. It's about raw, honest, heartfelt communication. Let your words flow freely; let them come straight from your heart.

"Let your heart guide your pen on this journey of healing. In every letter, every word, every memory shared, you're not just expressing your grief; you're honoring your love."

Michele Bell

7

AS WE DRAW TODAY'S LESSON TO A CLOSE, I INVITE YOU TO REFLECT ON THESE THREE CONSIDERATIONS:

Reflection: How did the process of writing the letter make you feel? Did it bring up any new emotions or insights about your grief?

_____

_____

_____

_____

Expression: Were any thoughts or feelings you found particularly challenging to express in your letter? How might you approach these in your future writing?

_____

_____

_____

_____

Connection: Did you feel connected with your loved one in writing the letter? How can you continue to nurture this connection in your healing journey?

_____

_____

_____

_____

"In every heartfelt letter, we find a bridge to our loved ones, a pathway to healing, and a testament to the enduring power of love."

Michele Bell

I encourage you to pen as many letters as your heart desires. As we conclude today's lesson, I invite you to take at least 60 seconds to CONNECT with the process. Remember, you're not just going through this process but actively shaping it. You are strong. You are powerful. You are in control. And above all, you are empowered.

LESSON 2 — Dealing *with* Change

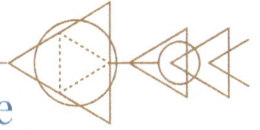

Every soul dances to the rhythm of loss in its unique way. For some, the dance begins abruptly, the music of loss striking a sudden, discordant note. The melody unfolds slowly for others, a haunting tune that lingers over time. Some of us, with an intuitive ear, can hear the faint strains of the song even before it fully begins.

Take a moment to remember when the music first reached you.

This moment, this first note of your loss, is the starting point of your journey. It's the foundation upon which you'll write your letters this week. It's the moment when the landscape of your life shifts, and the world takes on a different hue. Things will never be the same, and acknowledging this change is crucial to your healing process.

Take a moment to jot down any thoughts from this reflection.

Your memories are the melodies that will guide you on this journey. They are the notes that compose the song of your healing. Embrace them with resonance; they are the notes guiding you toward healing.

So, let the music play, let your pen dance on the paper, and let your healing journey begin.

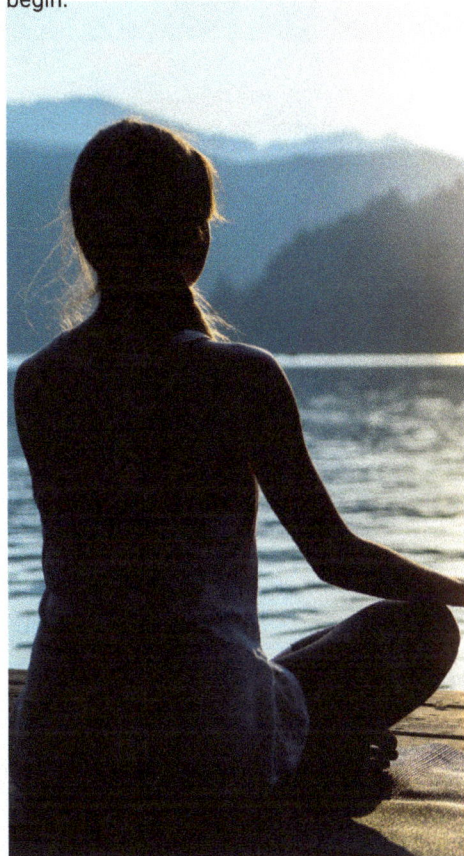

Navigating the Uncharted: Making Sense of Loss

Humans are wired to seek understanding and find patterns and logic in the world around us. Though small, our minds are vast in their capacity to problem-solve and guide us through life's challenges. We lean on our intellect in times of need, trusting it to illuminate our path.

Yet, it's important to remember that it's okay to feel lost and not to have all the answers. Grief is not a problem to be solved but a journey to be traveled. And as you journey through your loss, know that you are seen, you are heard, and you are not alone.

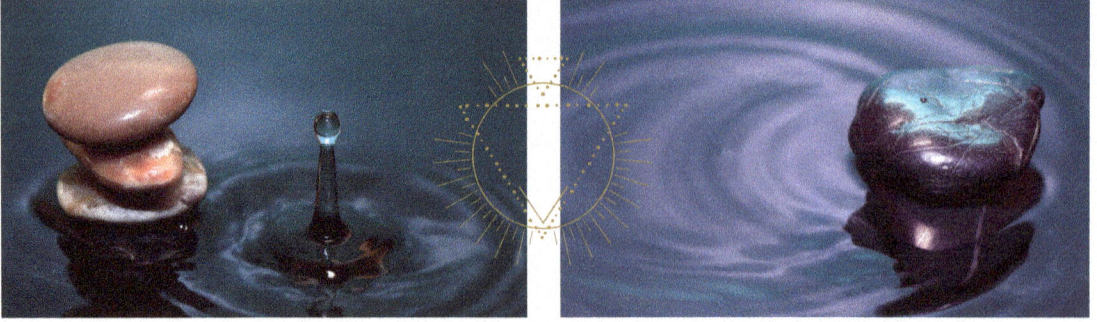

In the wake of grief, loss, and trauma, even your body may seem to retreat, conserving energy as it navigates the unfamiliar landscape of sorrow. You've witnessed a chapter of your life transition from the present to the past, a shift that can be challenging to comprehend. Many of us turn to a higher power, seeking solace in religious or spiritual beliefs during these times.

In its gentle rhythm, writing can serve as a beacon of light in these moments of darkness. It can help you:

- Understand Your Loss
- Find peace in your belief system
- Uncover the 'Why'
- Pause, Observe, Reflect, Heal

Your Spiritual Journey:

When you experience a sudden and extreme change, you must find a way to rebuild. However, writing can be a gateway to finding perspective. You can never find peace until you understand your loss.

For those with religious or spiritual beliefs, these can provide solace in times of need. Loss often unearths feelings we were unaware of, such as hidden regrets. On the other hand, you may find yourself without guilt, a fortunate position that brings its form of peace.

How do we cope when a loved one is no longer with us? The beauty of our human experience is that we can connect with those no longer physically present. Through our imagination and visions, we can engage in conversations, revisit shared experiences, and keep our memories alive. This doesn't signify madness but our deep human need for connection.

Writing to or about your loved one can provide immense comfort. It allows you to revisit cherished memories, find closure, and maintain a connection. Throughout this course, you'll be encouraged to use your imagination for healing and write letters that bridge the gap between loss and love.

Writing to your lost one or about them can be exceptionally comforting, giving you a sense of closure and looking back on fond memories. Remember, the path ahead is new, but you're not alone. Your feelings are seen, your experiences are valid, and your story matters.

Letters of Love

Take a deep breath, find a quiet space, and let your heart guide your pen. It's time to write a letter to your loved one. Begin with a simple, heartfelt salutation:
*Please find a photograph of your loved one and place it before you.

Dear _____, One feeling I've felt coming up a lot lately is...

_____
_____
_____
_____
_____
_____
_____
_____

As We Conclude Today's Journey, Reflect on These Three Considerations:

If I could forgive my loved one for something, it would be...

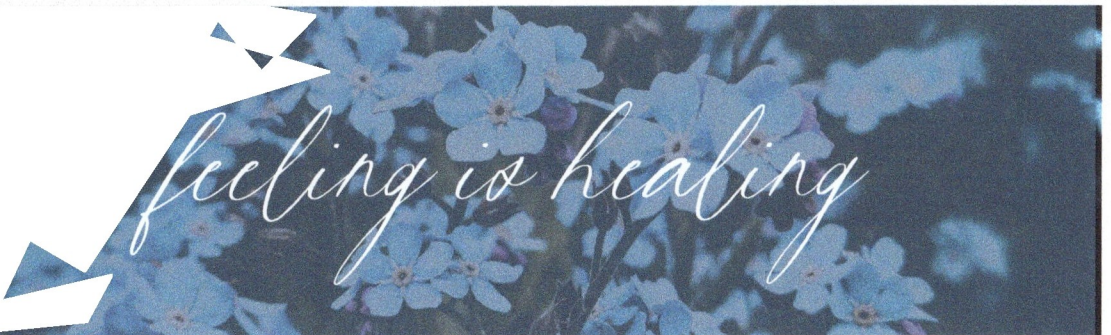

_____
_____
_____
_____

feeling is healing

If I could forgive myself for something, it would be...

_____

_____

_____

_____

_____

_____

_____

_____

How can you turn these raw emotions into a positive experience?

_____

_____

_____

_____

_____

_____

_____

_____

30 Days of Connection: A Healing Journey

For the next 30 days, write a letter to your loved one each morning and evening. Share your daily experiences, thoughts, and memories. On a full moon night, find a peaceful spot outdoors or create a serene space indoors with a white candle and an earthing mat. Read one of your letters aloud, imagining your loved one beside you, sharing this moment. Through this practice, you will feel seen, heard, and connected on your path to healing.

LESSON 3

Remembering Moments *before* Loss

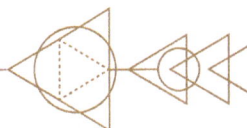

When we experience a loss, our initial state is usually shocking. Our minds struggle to comprehend the absence of someone or something significant, and we feel numb emotionally and physically. Expressing the loss in words can be difficult during the first few hours and days.

As we attempt to return to our daily routine, reminders of the loss can flood our minds unexpectedly and bring us back to despair. These memories contain messages that are crucial to our healing process. Ignoring them could lead us to get stuck in a cycle of grief. However, sharing these memories can give us the power to overcome our pain.

> *"Everybody needs his memories. They keep the wolf of insignificance from the door."*
>
> *K. R. Fischer*

Unearthing Memories: A Journey Through Time

As you allow memories to surface, you may experience some for the first time. However, most people dealing with loss will be able to name their repeated memories off the top of their heads. These memories often pop up regularly and can bring both pain and happiness. Pleasant and painful memories are equally important and worthy of being written about.

Take time, find a comfortable sitting spot, and reflect on your memories before experiencing a significant loss. What initially comes to mind? It's helpful to take note of these memories as they surface organically, without any pressure to force them.

In today's lesson, there won't be any letter-writing assignments. Instead, the task is to organize these memories in a natural order—in a way that feels natural to you. After you create a list of positive and negative recollections, please keep it in a safe place for future lessons. You are adding more nuggets to your journey!

Art Therapy Homework
7 day challenge

Here are the supplies you will need:

- Colored tissue paper, which you can use to represent the various emotions you are feeling now.
- A journal, scrapbook, or some paper.
- Colored markers.
- Glue, paintbrush, and glaze.

one

Create a list of emotions you are feeling. Some common grief emotions are despair, anxiety, guilt, anger, denial, fear, isolation, loneliness, sadness, numbness, etc. Positive emotions can be like joy, gratitude, love, and hope.

_____

_____

two

Tear off each colored tissue relating to the emotion you are feeling daily.

three

Write down the emotion next to the colored tissue paper.

four

Complete the entire page to represent the colors of emotions you are experiencing.

five

Be creative each day. Place into a collage. That's it! Glue and Glaze.

art therapy homework

This assignment helps create each day's page to represent the current combination of emotions you are experiencing. Morning or evening is recommended to commit yourself to this assignment.

It helps visually show the ebbs and flows of different emotions over time.

You can also create this design on an empty wall in your home!

Let your pen flow across your journal, each word a step towards healing.

What does moving toward your pain mean to you?

In our healing journey, we often encounter the concept of moving toward our pain. But what does this truly mean to you? This isn't about dwelling in sorrow but acknowledging it, understanding it, and learning from it.

Take a moment to reflect on this idea. **How do you perceive this movement toward your pain? What emotions or thoughts does it evoke?**

Consider a moment when you consciously chose to move toward your pain. **What did you learn from this experience? How did it contribute to your healing process?**

Remember, your perspective is unique and valuable. Through this reflection, you are seen and heard, and your experiences are acknowledged.

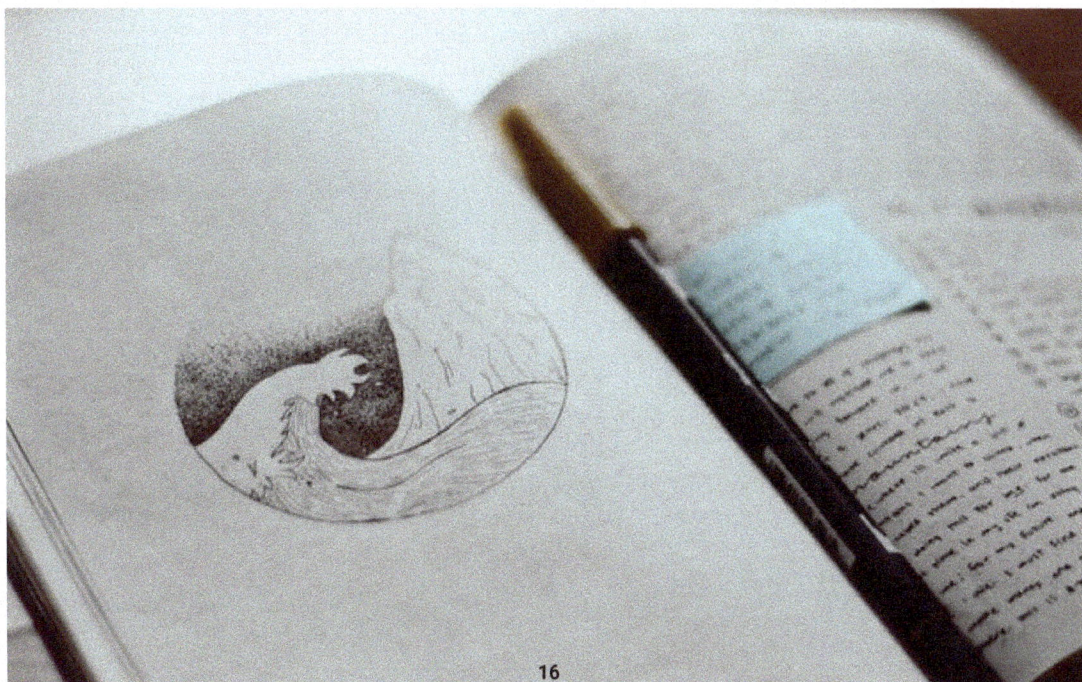

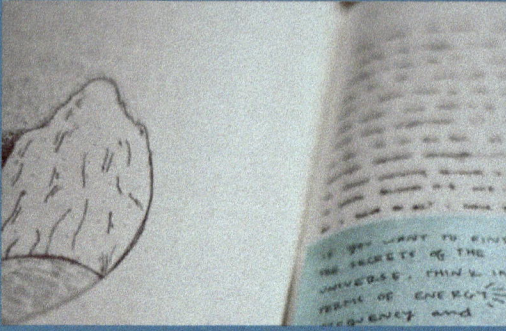

As you end each day's lesson, take a moment to reflect, an invitation to healing. Your grief, with its unique rhythm of pain, will continue to seek your attention, gently urging you to embrace it, bit by bit.

How is the pain of your grief seeking your attention?
In its profound depth, grief often communicates with us subtly. It nudges us, seeking our attention. **So, how is the pain of your grief reaching out to you?**
Take a moment to reflect on this. **Are there specific moments, thoughts, or feelings that amplify your grief? Are there certain triggers that bring your pain to the forefront?**

Remember, your grief is a part of your journey, not an obstacle to be overcome. You are taking a crucial step toward healing by acknowledging and understanding its signals.

List the changes you've noticed due to your current challenges.

These could be related to our sense of self, such as confidence, identity, health, or personality changes. They could impact our sense of security, affecting our emotional stability, financial situation, or lifestyle. They could even touch upon our understanding of meaning, altering our faith, dreams, goals, or joy.

Once you've identified these losses, choose one or two that resonate deeply with you. Write about each one, exploring their impact on your life and your feelings towards these changes.

Imagine you could ask these changes one question. What would it be?

Ask EACH change, "How can I learn to adapt to you?" or "What lessons are you here to teach me?" or even "How can I find peace between the twists and turns of these changes?"

LESSON 4

Dealing *with* Painful Memories

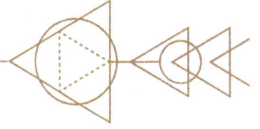

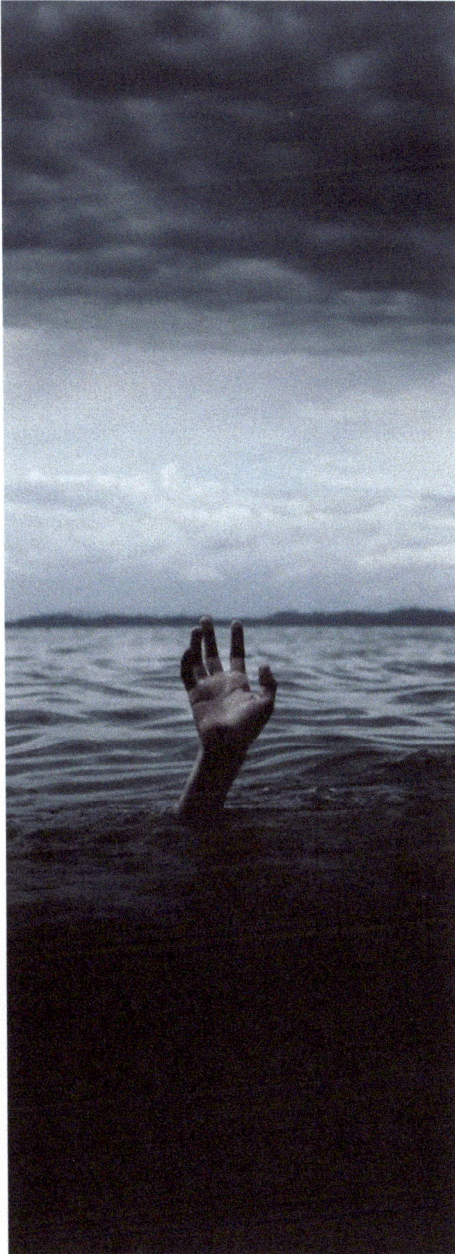

We've explored memories over the past three lessons, including some that may have caused us pain. We have also found that acknowledging and accepting these emotions can help lessen the pain. Writing to your loved ones and discussing these feelings and memories can bring comfort.

When we experience loss, some of us may want to forget, but another part of us may resist doing so. It's important to recognize that we can't truly move forward without releasing the pain, but that doesn't mean it's easy. Letting go of the pain can feel like letting go of the person, which can be confusing and overwhelming.

This can be an extremely confusing time. As we *move with*, please acknowledge any reluctance to let go of your writing if you feel the urge to. This is a reminder to be mindful of these feelings, as accepting them is an integral part of the creative and healing process. Take your time and allow yourself to find positivity in the healing process, which will ultimately help you move forward.

> "Pleasure is the flower that passes; remembrance, the lasting perfume."
>
> *Jean de Boufflers*

The Metamorphosis of Memories: From Sorrow to Serenity

Memories, even the most painful ones, can be rewritten. They can transform to evolve into something meaningful, even positive, over time.

Consider, for instance, the sudden loss of a family member in a car accident. The tragedy was so overwhelming that every car, every road became a stark reminder of the loss. Our shared love for automobiles, once a source of joy and connection, seemed to be overshadowed by the enormity of the grief.

Yet, as time passed and the raw edges of the loss began to soften, a shift occurred. You could revisit the cherished memories we had created together, tinkering with our grandfather's car in his old, dusty garage. The laughter, the camaraderie - these memories began to resurface, their light piercing through the veil of grief.

While still present, the loss sting wasn't as severe. The space created made room for positive memories, allowing them to coexist. This journey is a valuable lesson about the resilience of the human spirit and the importance of cherishing life's fleeting moments while we can.

In writing the therapeutic potential of writing is a well-documented phenomenon. Many renowned authors have attested to the role of writing in navigating their mental health journeys. Writing serves as a compass, guiding them through the complex maze of their emotions.

.

When confronted with a traumatic loss, our brain often captures a visual snapshot of the moment, a poignant still frame that the smallest things can trigger.

Yet, when we translate our experiences into words, we create a space to confront and understand our loss. Writing allows us to dissect our pain, view it from different angles, and, ultimately, lessen its impact.

If left unaddressed, the pain can continue to grow, casting a long shadow over our lives. But when we engage the written side of our brain, we initiate a healing process.

Words become our allies, helping us navigate the terrain of trauma and loss. Many have walked this path before us, and their experiences show us the incredible transformational power of writing.

Writing Memories

To minimize distractions, you may consider moving to a comfortable and safe space, like your sacred sanctuary. When you are ready to reminisce about your loved one, begin writing:

Dear _____, no matter how hard I try, I cannot forget this memory, and I wanted to talk to you today...

_____

_____

_____

_____

_____

_____

_____

_____

PLEASE USE A JOURNAL TO WRITE DOWN AN INTUITIVE PROMPT

As you conclude, pause and reflect on these three thoughts:
Reflect on the emotional landscape painted by their presence in your life.

I feel the strongest sense of connection with my loved one when....

_____

_____

_____

_____

_____

_____

_____

_____

Journey back to a moment shared with your loved one that sparked laughter. Can you recall the details of that moment? Where were you both? What words were spoken? What actions led to the outburst of joy?

_____
_____
_____
_____
_____
_____
_____
_____

How did the presence of your loved one stir emotions within you? Were there specific instances where their actions or words kindled a particular feeling?

_____
_____
_____
_____
_____
_____
_____
_____

If you have more than one memory to share today, feel free to write multiple letters in your journal. You can use the prompts given above to write another letter.

Writing is healing.

LESSON 5

Express What Your Loss Means *to* You

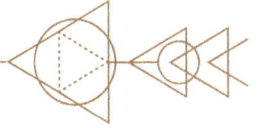

Navigating through the aftermath of a loss can feel like walking through a fog, where everything familiar suddenly becomes unclear. It's a harsh reminder of how quickly life can change and how joy can unexpectedly turn into sorrow. The absence left by losing someone or something important can create a deep sense of emptiness. But we begin to see the first signs of healing in recognizing this loss and facing this emptiness.

""Voicing the Significance of Your Loss is a Personal Reflection of Self"

Michele Bell

Take a moment to reflect on the depth of your loss. Beyond the irreplaceable individual, what else has been taken away? Are there emotional echoes that continue to resonate within you? Has it altered the rhythm of your daily life, reshaped your conversations, or changed your plans? As you journey through the grieving process, allow yourself to explore these aspects, for they, too, form part of your story of loss.

Life flashes by in an instant, so it is essential to take the time to enjoy the little things, like smelling the first flowers of spring. It can often feel like juggling many balls simultaneously while pausing to enjoy something else is seemingly impossible.

However, it is time for this lesson to put the balls down momentarily. This is about savoring those sweet smells.

Capturing precisely what you have lost in words is nearly impossible. There are so many things, memories, and emotions that cannot be described. It isn't just about who a person was to you; it is about how they enriched your life and the void they have left behind.

Of course, living with their essence every day was an effortless pleasure, but living without them is hard. Now it is time to let your loved one know it's not about how they died; it's about how they lived that brought JOY into your existence.

Use the following as a library of ideas to spark your memory.

The loss of a person/animal:

- The harmony you had
- How they improved your life
- How they helped
- How they hindered
- What you shared
- What conflicts you had
- What resolutions you found
- What you remember most

- First impression
- Final memory
- How did they make you proud?
- How did you make them proud?
- Something you never knew
- Something you wish you could ask
- The one thing you would do with them now

The loss of health:

- What you took for granted
- How you have changed since
- A gift from the loss
- Why it is hard to live without

- What you have learned from it
- What you would change
- What you can no longer do
- Advice for others

The loss of a job:

- What you lost
- Why you loved it
- Why you hated it
- What it gave you

- What you miss most
- What you have learned since
- What do you want next?

USE YOUR JOURNAL TO WRITE DOWN INTUITIVE PROMPTS

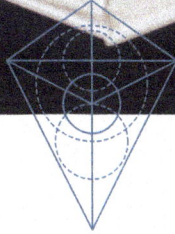

Jot down any memories triggered by these prompts and save them for future reference. These notes will be valuable when you write letters to departed loved ones, particularly when expressing gratitude for how they enhanced your life.

After going through a loss, reminiscing about memories, even happy ones, can be difficult and distressing. It requires effort to let go of the emotions that come with recalling the memory. But by articulating what they meant to you in words, you may preserve those memories close to your heart forever.

Personal Reflections

Find your tranquil sanctuary, a place free from interruptions. Prepare to delve into the following thoughts - close your eyes, take a calming breath...and let your writing journey begin.

Dear __________, you meant the world to me, during our shared moments, you made me feel...

Dear __________, your laughter, which still echoes in my mind, always made me...

Dear __________, I realize that you taught me...

As you conclude this letter, you are reminded of the strength of your bond, a connection that transcends physical presence. You are comforted by our shared love and memories.

____________, Until we meet again in my next letter, know you are forever in my heart.

PLEASE USE YOUR JOURNAL TO WRITE DOWN INTUITIVE PROMPTS

Before concluding, kindly take a moment...

I often think about what I would do differently with my loved one if I had the chance.
One of my favorite ideas is...

_____
_____
_____
_____
_____
_____
_____
_____

One thing I want to remember about you, one thing that I hold dear in my heart is...

_____
_____
_____
_____
_____
_____
_____
_____

Take a breath in between. If you need to write more, please feel free to do so. Please write as many letters as you need to move your feelings into a space of peace within; I hope you got this...

LESSON 6   Eliminated *Grief*

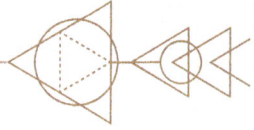

Over the past five lessons, you have expressed your loss in many ways. However, we have yet to discuss how loss manifests in the body. We have spoken about the link between body, mind, heart, and soul – each being as important as the other. If a loss impacts the reason, it also affects the other three. Therefore, caring for all parts of yourself is essential to maintaining a healthy lifestyle.

Typically, when people are asked to depict loss in the body, they may draw a broken heart, even though they understand that it's not physically torn. This illustrates how grief feels – like a sudden shock to the mind, confusion in the spirit, and pain in the heart. It's as if something crucial is missing from the body, creating a space in the heart.

In the past, if someone had mentioned feeling a hole in their heart due to loss, a doctor might have dismissed it as a mental issue. However, mind-body medicine has evolved significantly over the last two decades, as demonstrated by the phenomenon of ghost limbs, where amputees feel sensations in limbs they lost long ago. We now understand that the mind and body are intricately interconnected.

This can be linked to how the human heart misses a loved one. This "broken heart" feeling is more than just a metaphor. The emotional pain and stress that come with grief can trigger various physical symptoms, including chest pain, shortness of breath, and even changes in heart rhythm. This is due to the body's physiological response to intense emotions, potentially leading to a condition known as "broken heart syndrome" or Takotsubo cardiomyopathy.

Love is always connected to the heart; therefore, it is vulnerable when dealing with the loss of love. In a scientific sense, psychological responses are examples of the mind-body connection.

Not addressing grief can lead to serious conditions like depression and a lack of energy. That's why the 7 Stages of Grief were created with love and purpose.

Listen To Your Body:

Imagine your body as a vessel, a storyteller, whispering tales of your experiences, joys, and sorrows. When navigating the turbulent seas of grief, your body often becomes a lighthouse, signaling distress in its unique language. Writing, my dear reader, becomes a bridge, a translator, between you and your body's silent whispers. It's a proven salve, a balm that soothes the wounds of the heart, mind, and body.

Loss, you see, doesn't always echo in the heart's chambers. It can ripple out, touching every cell and every fiber of your being. It can sneak into your immune system, the body's fortress, and weaken defenses. Stress, the shadow of grief, can leave you vulnerable, especially if you're already grappling with health issues. Sometimes, it might even unmask a hidden ailment—a secret your body has kept.

Now, I don't mean to alarm you but rather to awaken you to the wisdom of your body. To help you understand its signals, listen to its stories.

Once you decipher how grief has etched itself into your physical being, you can start expressing it and releasing the pain. Writing about this pain can pave the path to healing and connection, regardless of distance.

So, let's embark on this journey together, pen in hand, ready to listen to our bodies' stories.

28

Message in a Bottle

Your body is a vessel carrying messages from your heart. It's like a bottle floating in the sea of your emotions, filled with words unsaid, feelings unfelt.

What physical sensations or changes have you noticed since your loss?

Write a letter to your loved one, sharing these observations as if they were messages in a bottle, cast into the sea of your shared memories.

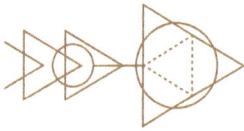

Stress, the shadow of grief, can leave imprints on your body. It's as if each wave of grief etches a message onto the bottle of your body.

How has stress manifested in your physical well-being? In your letter, describe these manifestations as messages etched onto a bottle, waiting to be discovered and understood.

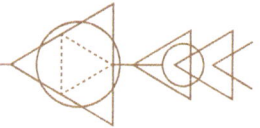

Writing about your pain can pave the path to healing, like a message in a bottle reaching your loved one.

What healing messages would you want to send to your loved one about your journey through grief? In your letter, imagine placing these healing messages into a bottle, letting them float across the sea of time and space to reach your loved one.

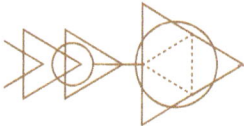

Write down whatever comes to mind without analyzing. Just let the pain speak for itself. Be Present with the physical connection to your grief as you write.

PLEASE USE YOUR JOURNAL TO WRITE YOUR THOUGHTS AND MESSAGES

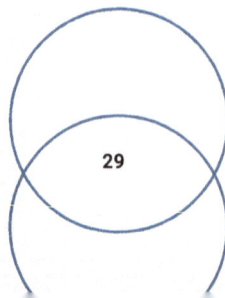

29

As we draw this chapter to a close, I invite you to pause and reflect on the following three questions

What emotions surfaced as you wrote your 'message in a bottle' to your loved one?

_____

_____

_____

_____

_____

_____

How has this exercise of writing letters to your loved one influenced your perspective on your grief journey?

_____

_____

_____

_____

_____

_____

What is one thing you learned about yourself through this process that you weren't aware of before?

_____

_____

_____

_____

_____

_____

If you feel the urge to write more, go ahead. Expressing your physical discomfort can bring relief and help you tune into your body's signals. Pay attention to what your body tells you and address concerns quickly to enhance your recovery. Treating your body with kindness and attentiveness is a vital part of self-care.

LESSON 7

Taking Notices *of* Coincidences

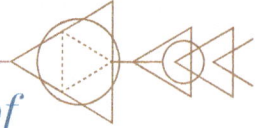

Let's discuss the mysterious realm beyond the veil, invisible to us but where departed loved ones reside. Even though we cannot see them, we can still sense their presence. When we put our feelings of loss into words, we create a heartfelt and enduring memorial. Grief is a complex emotion that grows without a cure. It goes beyond the limits of the body and the mind, hitting our very essence at the level of the soul and the heart.

EXPRESS is a philosophy that promotes candid discussions about death and dying. While it cannot eliminate the anguish of losing a loved one, it helps reduce the shame, fear, confusion, and stigma associated with grief. It is possible to find significance in our suffering.

I want you to throw yourself headfirst into this writing process. Give your mind permission to wander aimlessly into the unknown. If you keep digging, you might find something that helps you feel better. Keep an open mind and rely on your instincts. Do what is right for you, following your moral compass.

> *"A coincidence is an illuminating moment, reaching for the message in synchronicity beyond the veil."*
>
> *The Grief Warrior*

Embracing the Heart's Vision

Your mind, while powerful, is not the sole healer in times of loss. Logic alone cannot foster the connection you seek with your departed loved ones. The manner of their presence may remain a mystery, but their appearance in your life is a certainty. Writing letters to them can be a profound way to sense their enduring presence. Surrender to the longing for connection and remain receptive.

Beyond the Veil: Continuing the Conversation

Even in their absence, your loved ones can communicate their closeness to you. This communication can manifest in myriad ways, but there are certain consistent signs that you can trust, provided you are open to receiving and ready to embrace these messages from beyond the veil.

Sensing their Presence

The Physical Connection: You may experience a physical reaction, such as the hairs on your neck standing on end, signaling their closeness. Have faith in your inner knowing to identify these times, decipher the context, and know when they are near.

Serendipity: The Power of Happenstance

In the grand scheme of things, timing and location are everything. It likely is if an occurrence feels like an encounter with a departed loved one. If anything feels like meeting a dead relative, it probably is. Examples include seeing a prophetic sign at a loved one's funeral or running into a poignant reminder on a major anniversary. Sometimes, these deeply personal and perfectly timed signs are too profound to overlook. Rather than trying to orchestrate these happy coincidences, allow yourself to appreciate them when they organically unfold.

Here are some of the most common ones that people experience:

LIGHT

Illuminated Memories:
Light in the Shadows of Loss.
Peculiar lights or orbs in photos or
flickering of lights.

BUTTERFLY

A symbol of metamorphosis is
when the spirit leaves the body.
This transformation is not an
ending but a transition - a change
in state rather than a cessation.

DREAMS

Comfort in Slumber's Embrace:
Nocturnal encounters can provide
solace, healing, and a sense of
continued connection.

RAINBOWS

Serendipitous Sightings: Love's enduring symbols.

SOUND

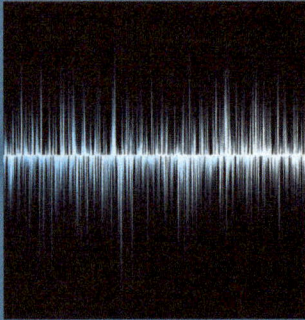

Echoes of the Heart: Voices and melodies from beyond.

ANIMALS

Feathered Messengers: Birds as symbols of hope and positivity.

TOUCH

The Unseen Embrace: A mysterious touch from a loved one.

OBJECTS

It is finding an item that feels like it was put there by your loved one.

SMELLS

Your loved one's natural smell, a fragrance they used to wear, and their favorite flower are all common signs.

Observing the experiences of others who have gone through a similar loss can be beneficial to gain insight into what may be possible for your own healing journey. Try using theta meditation first thing in the morning to train your mind to be open and accepting.

Be accepting of yourself and others as you recover. Positive developments can show themselves in various ways, some more noticeable than others. The recovery process can be tremendously aided by maintaining awareness and openness to these shifts.

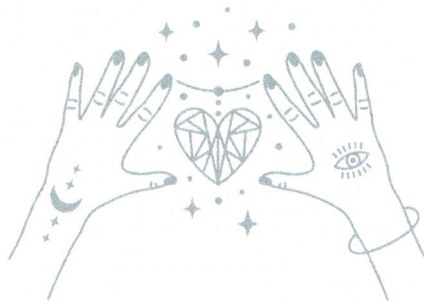

Heart2Heart

Try penning a letter to yourself—just not from your own point of view. Try writing it from your loved one's point of view instead. Allow their words of love and encouragement to flow from their heart through your fingertips and onto paper.

What do they think they'd say? Can you imagine any words of solace or support they might say? How would they constantly remind you of your undying love for one another?

This is not an opportunity for fantasy or wishful thinking. It's a method to reconnect with the unconditional love that your departed friend or family member gave you. So let this letter represent their words, a symbol of their love, and a reminder of the strength of your relationship.

Dear (Your Name), If your loved one did anything to inspire you, what was it?

_____

_____

_____

_____

_____

_____

_____

_____

_____

_____

_____

_____

_____

Put your reaction and feelings into words as best you can. Write from the heart and be authentic. Let your loved one know everything you have to express.

Before you conclude this heartfelt exercise, pause and reflect.
Ask yourself these soul-searching questions:

What are the unique qualities, gestures, or moments that you deeply miss about your loved one?

_____
_____
_____
_____
_____
_____

Is there a recent event, a milestone, or a simple everyday occurrence you wish to share with them?

_____
_____
_____
_____
_____
_____

Have you recently noticed coincidences that remind you of your loved one? Please elaborate.

_____
_____
_____
_____
_____
_____

PLEASE USE YOUR JOURNAL TO WRITE DOWN YOUR THOUGHTS

LESSON 8

A Message *from* Your Loved One

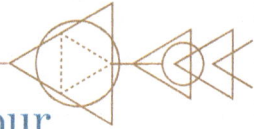

This is a sacred space where we'll explore the profound and mysterious ways our departed loved ones still speak to us.

Could our loved ones communicate with us through an unbreakable cord of love that transcends death?

Listen with an open heart for messages from loved ones who have crossed over to the other side, *beyond the veil*. They want to be heard; all we have to do is *pay attention*.

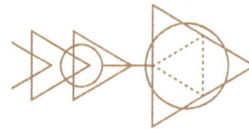

Voices Beyond the Veil: Understanding Messages from Loved Ones

In the quiet corners of our everyday lives, there exists a gentle hum, a whispering echo that resonates from a world beyond our own. These are the dimensions from which our departed loved ones communicate with us.

Imagine a familiar tune playing when you're thinking of them or a vivid dream that feels like a visit. These aren't mere coincidences but meaningful messages from beyond the veil.

These moments, these messages, are not mere figments of our imagination. They are tangible signs from our loved ones, assuring us of their continued existence in different forms and dimensions. These transmissions can be as brief as a butterfly's wingbeat or as soft as a feather's touch. In our dreams, our departed loved ones can visit us, their words and deeds as meaningful and kind as they were in life.

You will learn to trust and trust these clues along the way. You will learn how our loved ones reach out to us, providing comfort, love, and the certainty that the physical world does not bind the bond.

Let's journey together, listening to the whispers of the unseen. The limitless strength of love will be on full display for all to see. We will explore the peace and security of knowing loved ones are never far away.

The Inner Voice

The Inner Voice echoes the presence of our loved ones. This lesson is a testament to the power of memory and the enduring bonds of love that transcends physical presence.

To prepare for this task, gather items that remind you of your loved one. This could be photographs, letters, artwork, or any object that holds a special significance. Spend time with these items, let them stir your memories, and awaken the senses connecting you to your loved one.

Take a moment to immerse yourself in these reminders. Try to recall the sounds of their laughter, the scent that was uniquely theirs, the warmth of their touch, or the comfort of their presence.

Now, bring these items where you feel comfortable and ready to write. Let these objects serve as silent conversationalists, their energy contributing to the narrative you're about to weave. Creating an altar will enhance the power to receive...

Let "The Inner Voice" guide your words as you write in this lesson. This voice imbued with the essence of your loved one, will lend authenticity to your writing. Remember, the more your writing resonates with their voice, the more healing the process will be.

Postcards to the Stars: Expressing What Can't Be Said

This is your opportunity to articulate those sentiments that have yet to be voiced, to bridge the gap between the here and the beyond. Before your pen touches the paper, close your eyes.

Visualize your loved one. Recall the sound of their laughter, the warmth of their gaze, the comfort of their presence. Hold these memories close as you prepare to write.

Launch into your letter. Let the words pour out of you as you write their name, evoking their very being on the page. Share with them the moments of your life they've missed, the dreams you're chasing, the struggles you're encountering.

Express those unvoiced sentiments. Maybe it's a birthday greeting you forgot to send, an apology you had to postpone, or just a declaration of your undying love. Fill your "Postcard to the Stars" using these words.

Once you have finished writing your letter, you may just read it out loud. Allow your words to fill the room, giving your loved one's memory a place to flourish.

Remember, this is your letter, your connection to your loved one. There's no right or wrong way to do this. It's about giving voice to your heart's unspoken words, about keeping the bond alive, even across the stars.

As you conclude this exercise, gently ponder over these two questions.

What emotions surfaced as you penned this letter? Reflect on their role in your healing journey.

_____

_____

_____

_____

_____

_____

_____

_____

Did writing this letter bring any sense of relief or closure? Consider its impact on your journey toward peace.

_____

_____

_____

_____

_____

_____

_____

_____

PLEASE USE YOUR JOURNAL TO EXPRESS THESE THOUGHTS

Feel free to continue writing if you have more to say. You can even revisit your previous letters and respond to them if it feels appropriate. Stay open-minded and allow yourself to fully immerse in this experience. Consider creating a ritual to release any negative emotions and listen to your inner voice.

LESSON 9

The Burning Letter Ritual *for* Release

I love the use of rituals. Rituals cause us to take pause, giving weight to things that are significant to us. Rituals help us concentrate, stay present, and provide a sense of emotional and spiritual grounding. One such ritual that has been used historically for release is burning.

Nothing is more disruptive than the death of someone you love who intertwines with your being. When those people die, we are left floundering. The degree of connection you had with the deceased, whether spiritual, emotional, or physical, and how you view your existence both impact how intense your grief is. The stronger the bond you share, the more profound the impact of their death on your grieving process.

On my son's 36th birthday, memories flooded my mind as I embarked on a poignant ritual. It had been 17 years since he transitioned, and I felt compelled to let go of the weight that had clung to my heart. In the tranquil surroundings of my ancestral home, I set up a cauldron borrowed from my kitchen, ready to burn the remnants of the past. Sipping champagne, I settled on the grass, watching as the flames danced in hues of purple and yellow. With each funeral memento, I fed into the fire, my heavy heart became fleeting. These moments of emotional liberation held profound significance on my journey, nourishing the depths of my inner being.

Find a photograph of your loved one, place it before you, and light a candle. As you gaze into the flame, envision it as an illuminating guide for them to come to you. It is powerful to embrace your feelings, summon your memories, and invite them into your space.

The Palo Santo is burned before the ritual to purify the surroundings. You can use a fireproof bowl chosen explicitly for the burning ceremony, which holds sentimental value, or any vessel you already own—performing the ritual in a serene location where you can sit undisturbed, preferably outdoors in nature.

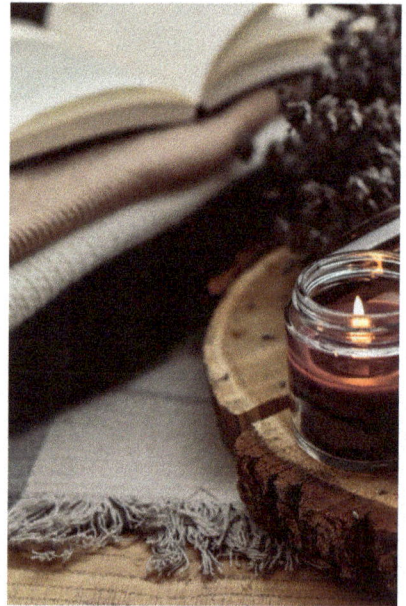

Full Moon Ritual

It's important to feel comfortable reading out loud.
The point is to read the letter out loud to your loved one to sense a connection. Why does this matter? When you read aloud, you fill your voice with energy, express your feelings through your words, and give them life. Take your time to facilitate emotional healing. If you're feeling overwhelmed, give yourself some time to recover. Feel free to express your feelings, whether tears of joy or laughter to the sky. If you're feeling overwhelmed, give yourself some time to recover. Don't be afraid to show your emotions by crying tears of joy or laughing until you hurt.

Prepare yourself to release your loved one to the universe.
Once you have read your letter aloud, hold it close to you. Take some time to reflect on what you have read and cherish the memories. When ready, hold the letter out and release your loved one by saying, "I release [name of a loved one] and their energy from my life. I am grateful for the time we spent together. With love, I release with gratitude. I release with love. I will release you to the universe and begin my healing journey."

Embracing Release: A Ritual of Purging and Remembrance
First, while holding the letter, fold it away from you to "let go" of the contents. Then, fold the letter outward as if presenting it as an offering to the infinite space of the universe. Turn the letter counterclockwise three times to imbue it with a spirit of letting go. Put the letter inside a fireproof container and light it with care. Watch in silence as the fire consumes the letter. Allow happy memories of your loved one to arise at this sacred time, welcoming the cleansing process with open arms.

Honoring the Ashes: A Choice of Resting Place
Once the letter has been transformed into ashes, a decision awaits on how to honor their presence. You can scatter the ashes in a cherished corner of your yard, allowing them to blend with the earth. Alternatively, you may bury them, providing a permanent resting place. Another possibility is to release the ashes to the whims of the wind, allowing nature to guide their dispersal. If you feel compelled to keep the ashes, they can be saved in an urn until the perfect location for scattering or safekeeping reveals itself. The choice is yours, guided by your profound connection with your loved one.

Reverent Cleansing of the Fireproof Bowl
It is time to pay attention to the fireproof bowl holding the transformative flames. Approach this task with intention, taking your time to ensure thorough cleansing. Let it symbolize closure and renewal, preparing the fireproof bowl for future journeys of remembrance and catharsis.

Filling the Void with Positive Energy
Choose a mantra that resonates deeply with you and invokes positive emotions and associations. Visualize this chosen mantra as an inspiration of positive energy, drawing it into the void left behind by grief.

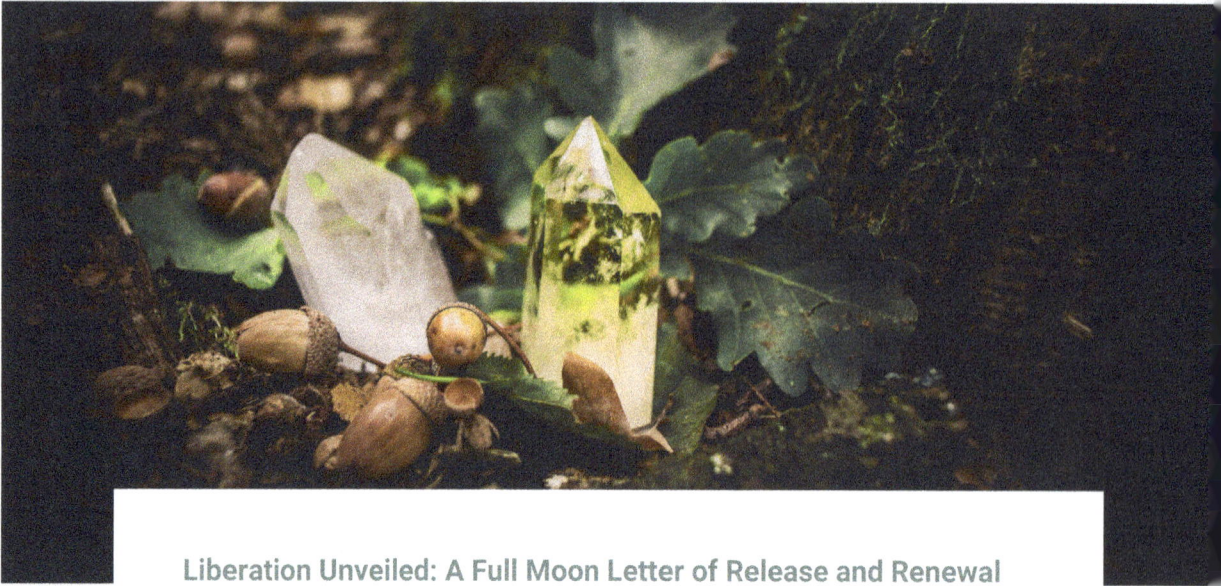

Liberation Unveiled: A Full Moon Letter of Release and Renewal

As the full moon graces the night sky, we invite you to embark on a transformative journey of realization and letting go. Let us begin this ritual with a proud bow to your unwavering courage.

Dear _____,

Writing this letter has triggered a flood of wonderful memories from our time together. I can still feel your presence, influencing my actions and inspiring my feelings. Pieces of our shared joy and love are woven together in my heart like a beautiful tapestry. My heart is heavy, but I am grateful for the time we shared; therefore, I am writing down my love, thankfulness, and gratitude for you.

In the depths of remembrance, I discover a wellspring of strength. Even in your absence, your grace remains a source of inspiration. As I navigate this path of recollection, I lovingly ask for your gentle guidance. Help me move forward with reverence, carrying the essence of our connection in every step I take.

With love and gratitude,

_____

WRITE THIS LETTER INTO YOUR JOURNAL

Feel free to continue writing if you have more to say. You can even revisit your previous letters and respond to them if it feels appropriate. Stay open-minded and allow yourself to fully immerse in this experience. Consider creating a ritual to release any negative emotions and listen to your inner voice.

In the tapestry of life, the grief journey tells a captivating tale, where *love and strength* emerge as the resilient threads that mend the heart.

The Grief Warrior

LESSON 10

The Power of
Connection *and* Healing

Reflecting on the Journey

Now that the course has concluded, a new chapter unfolds in your journey of healing and connection with your lost loved one. As we reflect on the transformative path we've walked together, let us delve into the significance of time and its profound impact on our well-being. It is often said that time can heal all things, but we have learned that time alone is not enough. Intentionally investing time in healing and self-care can expedite healing and transformation.

⊰⊱

In this final chapter, I invite you to engage in an interactive closing engagement, where we will explore a series of questions and prompts to deepen your connection with your loved one and foster healing in your life. By taking these deliberate steps towards communication and healing, we hope this journey has been helpful and profoundly meaningful to your life.

How would you describe your heart and emotions when you first started?

- How has this course impacted your understanding of grief and loss?
- What are some key insights or realizations you have gained along the way?
- Share a specific moment or exercise that significantly impacted your healing process.

How have your beliefs served you when you first started? And now?

- What steps will you take to initiate communication with your loved one?
- How do you envision these conversations or connections unfolding?
- Are there any specific messages or sentiments you wish to EXPRESS?

How are you doing mentally in the present day? Do you feel lighter?

- What self-care practices or rituals will you prioritize to support your healing journey?
- How can you create a safe and nurturing space for yourself to process your emotions?
- Are there any additional resources or support systems you plan to explore?

Have you noticed any healing or growth in your heart and emotional well-being?

- Reflect on the shifts and changes you have experienced since the beginning of this journey.
- Are there specific practices or moments contributing to this feeling of lightness?

Integration and Moving Forward:

- How do you plan to integrate the lessons and insights gained from this course into your daily life?
- What actions or changes are you inspired to make to live a more meaningful and fulfilling life?
- In what ways will you carry the memories and essence of your lost loved one as you move forward?

As you engage with these questions and prompts, trust in the wisdom within you. This closing engagement is an opportunity for introspection, growth, and intention setting. Remember, this is not the end but a continuation of your journey toward healing and connection.

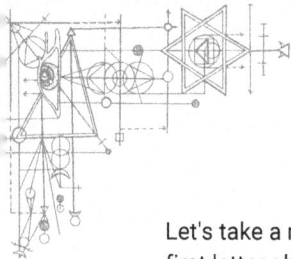

Let's take a moment to reflect on the first lesson and the experience of writing your first letter about a positive memory. Recall the emotions and sensations that arose as you put pen to paper and allowed the words to flow.

What was your favorite letter and why?
- Reflect on the various letters you have written since the beginning of this journey.
- Consider which letter resonated with you the most or made a deep connection.

How did your favorite letter make you feel?
- Describe the emotions and sensations that emerged as you crafted this letter.
- Did it evoke a profound sense of joy, healing, or nostalgia?
- Explore the impact this letter had on your overall well-being and inner state.

How did writing contribute to any changes in your memories?
- Describe the effects of writing on your overall recollection and interpretation of the past.
- Consider how introspection and putting thoughts into words impacted your understanding.

Have these changes in your memories brought about any shifts in your emotional well-being?
- Explore the connection between the evolving nature of your memories and your emotional state.
- Reflect on any emotional transformations that have occurred as a result of writing about your memories.

Did you learn anything new about your relationship with your loved one?
- Reflect on the letters and reflections you have written throughout this journey.
- Explore any newfound understanding of the dynamics, emotions, or aspects of your connection with your loved one.

Did writing help you set boundaries with family or friends?
- Reflect on your writing journey and the topics you have explored.
- Explore whether writing provided clarity, assertiveness, or a sense of empowerment in setting boundaries.

Did you feel the one you lost was close at any point?
- Reflect on your experiences throughout the ritual writing.
- Recall moments when you sensed the presence or connection of your loved one.

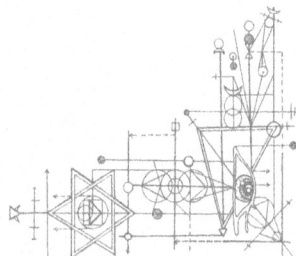

How did you know that the one you lost was close?
- o Describe the specific cues, experiences, or intuitions that made you feel their presence.
- o Did you notice any synchronicities, vivid dreams, or unexplainable occurrences that evoked a sense of their closeness?

If you had the opportunity to ask your loved one who has passed away one last question, what would it be, and why is it important to you?

Through this transformative journey, you have granted yourself the invaluable gift of time and space to heal and reconnect with what you have lost. You have navigated the depths of pain and emptiness, emerging stronger and wiser. Your letters have woven a powerful narrative of love, loss, and healing, a testament to your resilience and courage. The strength of the written word, the breadth of your imagination, and the enduring force of love have propelled you forward with each pen stroke as you begin the next chapter of your life. Your journey is truly inspiring.

"Our sorrows and wounds are healed only when we touch them with compassion."

Buddha

With heartfelt wishes for your continued growth and fulfillment, I am grateful for holding your heart on this transformative exploration. May the lessons embrace and the connections enrich your life, and may you find solace and healing in the profound power of love and remembrance.

I want you to know how much I appreciate your strength and perseverance as we close this chapter.

Writing Homework

Find your usual spot, embracing the stillness surrounding your rejuvenated spirit as you embark on this final letter with reverence and reflection.

My dearest (loved one), it has truly been an amazing journey. From the moment I wrote that very first letter, I never could have imagined...

_____

_____

_____

_____

_____

_____

_____

_____

Beloved Warriors,

As you have journeyed through our first stage, EXPRESS, I am reminded of the strength we endure each day. In your commitment to this exploration, you display courage — of inner quests. Each emotion and story written is a chapter in the grand narrative you're weaving.

The EMBRACE framework is a humble guide towards healing, understanding, and illuminating the way for yourself and others.

"In seeking, we often find in healing ourselves, we light the way for others."

With Healing Intention Always, MiMi

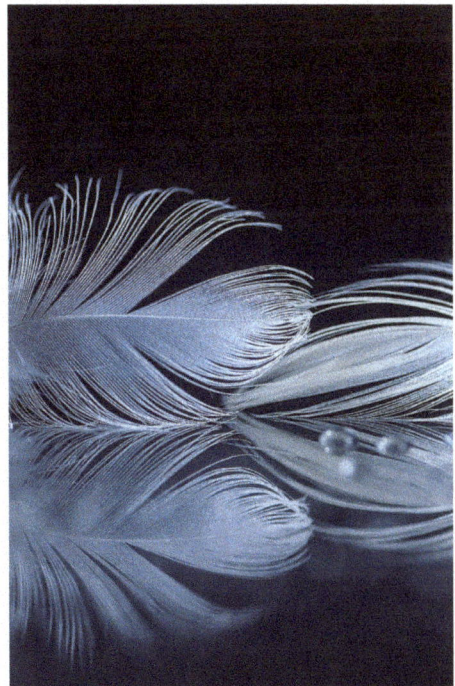

Michele C. Bell's narrative is a profound testament to resilience, the transformative power of embracing life's most profound challenges, and the depth of human compassion. Her journey, which began with the deeply personal and original work "*A Journey of Unconditional Love*," evolved into the 22-time award-winning story, "*A Son's Gift*," marking the inception of her distinguished career as an empathetic voice within the realm of grief literature.

With a Ph.D. in Philosophy and Metaphysics, Michele brings a unique blend of intuitive insight and scholarly depth to "*The 7 Stages of Grief* - **EMBRACE**." This work, unlike traditional grief literature, opens a space where healing is interwoven with personal growth and transformation, guided by Michele's own experiences, her profound journey through PTSD, and her scholarly insights. This journey has not only deepened her understanding of grief and resilience but also infused her writing with authenticity and compassion, offering solace and a transformative roadmap to those navigating the intricacies of loss.

Her innovative approach, blending the profound depths of intuitive philosophy with avant-garde grief counseling modalities, pioneers a novel paradigm in grief literature. Michele's work, transcending meticulous writing and exploration, charts a path towards transformative healing. Each stage, encapsulated within the evocative acronym **EMBRACE**, is meticulously crafted to guide the bereaved with dignity, offering nuanced understanding through the labyrinth of loss.

Beyond her literary contributions, Michele's life story—marked by resilience amidst adversity—enriches her professional narrative. From facing challenges such as bullying and domestic abuse to navigating the complexities of being a holistic real estate broker, Michele's experiences underscore her innate desire to support individuals through significant life transitions. The profound loss of her son to Ewings Sarcoma tested her resolve, catalyzing a shift towards mental health advocacy and the development of groundbreaking methodologies like the Soul Design technique and the *7 Stages of Grief* workbooks.

Michele's contributions extend to her active involvement in suicide prevention and domestic abuse programs, where her voice has become a force for change. Her purpose, whether as a holistic real estate broker, end-of-life expert, or mental health advocate, remains consistent—to support, guide, and uplift. As a member and keynote speaker for the **Daughters of Penelope**, Michele shares inspiring messages of healing, humor, and love, emphasizing the necessity of such virtues in today's world.

At 58, Michele C. Bell, The Grief Warrior®, stands as a testament to the enduring power of the human spirit, commanding respect and fostering deep, authentic connections. Her life experiences, granting her the invaluable CAT credentials of **Compassion, Authenticity, and Trust**, continue to inspire those fortunate enough to encounter her legacy..

Testimonial

In the wake of losing my niece, who was both an integral part of our family business and my daily life, I was engulfed by survivor's guilt and a maelstrom of emotions. At 74, having built a successful business career, I was unprepared for the profound impact this tragedy would have. The accident that took her life left me alone with my grief and a host of unresolved feelings, including an intense rage and sadness.

Then, I encountered Michele. She introduced me to a world of grace and dignity I hadn't known was possible. She guided me through techniques to stay ahead of depression, reduce stress, and embrace the present—prayer, meditation, and deep, conscious breathing became part of my routine. Her 30-day challenges and the comprehensive support she provided, spanning personal loss to business strategies, were transformative.

But Michele's impact didn't stop there. She introduced me to her eating healthy modality—incorporating balanced diets, regular exercise, and supplements into my daily regimen. These changes, under her guidance, not only improved my mental clarity but also led to significant weight loss and helped me stop drinking. Michele's approach broke me down and rebuilt me, a process my family witnessed as I underwent these massive shifts.

This woman has led me to a profound state of gratitude. Through her encouragement to write letters and share my deepest thoughts in a safe and authentic space, I found a unique kind of healing. Michele has restored joy to my life, demonstrating that even at this age, profound transformation is possible. Her expertise and genuine presence have given me back to myself, and family healthier and more vibrant. I stand in humble acknowledgment of the incredible journey she has guided me through.

Mike

DISCLAIMER

All content within the 7 Stages of Grief Alignment Workbook is original and intended solely to promote mind, body, and spirit well-being. This material does not replace the expertise or advice of a licensed mental health professional. Grief experiences are unique to each individual, and while the workbook provides supportive tools and perspectives, it does not guarantee specific outcomes. If you are experiencing intense or extreme distress, please consult a professional.

By using this course, you acknowledge and accept these terms and conditions. The 7 Stages of Grief certification program, conceived and developed by Dr. Michele Bell, offers an innovative, holistic, and empathy-driven approach to understanding and navigating grief. It is rooted in comprehensive research and deep insight into the human experience of loss and recovery.

Program Overview:
- Embracing Growth in Grief: Recognize the transformative potential within grief.
- The 7 Stages of Grief: Explore the intricate emotional journey of grief, encompassing its multifaceted seven stages.
- Pivoting with Purpose: Equip yourself with practical tools to channel grief's raw energy into purposeful action.
- Understanding the Power of Resistance: Gain insights into the obstacles resistance can pose on the healing journey and learn strategies to address and overcome it.
- Coping Modalities: Discover and apply various coping methods tailored to individual grief journeys or to assist others on this path.
- Certification: As a culmination, the program offers a certification examination to ensure a comprehensive understanding of the 7 Stages of Grief methodology.

Engage with the 7 Stages of Grief, All-In-One Master Compilation program to acquire a compassionate and informed approach to navigating the intricate labyrinth of grief, whether for personal growth or as a professional commitment.

Remember, every voice matters in bringing light to the shadows of grief. By uniting, we can raise awareness and create a world where everyone feels understood and supported during their moments of profound loss. I deeply appreciate your commitment to this cause. Please take a moment to sign the **Loss Awareness Day** petition on **Change.org**, inspired by the heartfelt endeavors of Lisa Marie Presley. Together, we can make a difference.
With heartfelt gratitude and hope,
MiMi + The Grief Warrior ®

www.ingramcontent.com/pod-product-compliance
Lightning Source LLC
Chambersburg PA
CBHW042336030426
42335CB00028B/3360